Tailored resources for better grades

MAKE THE GRADE

WJEC GCSE
English and English Language

Paula Adair

Foundation

Consultant: **Stuart Sage**

Revision Workbook

www.pearsonschoolsandfecolleges.co.uk
✓ Free online support
✓ Useful weblinks
✓ 24 hour online ordering
0845 630 33 33

Heinemann
Part of Pearson

D0241508

Heinemann is an imprint of Pearson Education Limited, a company incorporated in England and Wales, having its registered office at Edinburgh Gate, Harlow, Essex, CM20 2JE. Registered company number: 872828

www.pearsonschoolsandfecolleges.co.uk

Heinemann is a registered trademark of Pearson Education Limited

Text © Pearson Education Limited 2011

First published 2011

15 14 13 12 11
10 9 8 7 6 5 4 3 2 1

British Library Cataloguing in Publication Data
A catalogue record for this book is available from the British Library

ISBN 978 0 435027 55 1

Websites
The websites used in this book were correct and up-to-date at the time of publication. It is essential for tutors to preview each website before using it in class so as to ensure that the URL is still accurate, relevant and appropriate.

Edited by Julia Naughton
Designed and produced by Kamae Design, Oxford
Cover design by Wooden Ark Studios, Leeds
Original illustrations © Pearson Education Limited 2011
Picture research by Elena Wright
Cover photo © SA TEAM/FN/Minden/FLPA
Printed in Spain by Grafos, Barcelona

Acknowledgements
The authors and publisher would like to thank the following individuals and organisations for permission to reproduce material in this book:

P4 extracts from Bristol Zoo Gardens leaflet. Reprinted with kind permission. P6 extracts from 'What a waste!' produced by Mid Sussex District Council, used with kind permission. P8 'Piling Up Problems' by David Derbyshire, Daily Mail, 20th April 1998. Reprinted with permission of Solo Syndications. P12 'Please Will You Stop Paying To Have My People Murdered?' article. Reprinted with kind permission of Friends of the Earth. P14 'The Effects of a _Pack of 20 on an Expectant Mother' produced by IFAW. Reprinted with permission. P17 'Why we all hate Jamie Oliver' by Mecca Ibrahim © Mecca Ibrahim. Reprinted with kind permission of the author. P25 'Your weight and BMI' article from www.youngwomenshealth.org © 2010 Center for Young Women's Health, Children's Hospital Boston. All rights reserved. Used with permission. P27 Cenarth Adventure Centre leaflet, reprinted with permission. PP32-33 'The Polar Bears of Churchill' from www.wildlifeadventures.com. Reprinted with kind permission. P40 'Marchants Hill' brochure extract from PGL Adventure Holidays www.pgl.co.uk. Reprinted with kind permission. P41 'Home or Away?' extracts adapted from PGL Parent by Andrew Purvis, The Observer, 30th August 1998 © Guardian News and Media Ltd 1998. Reprinted with permission. P45 The 'Banana Campaign sheet'. Reprinted with permission of Fairtrade Foundation. P46 'We're all going bananas' by Robin McKie, from The Observer, 30th June 2002 © Guardian News & Media Lid 2002. Reprinted with permission. P82 'Drink, Drugs and Sausage Rolls' extract. Reprinted with permission. P84 'Getting Active Feeling Fit' © Crown Copyright 2007. Crown Copyright material is reproduced by the permission of the Controller of HMSO and Queen's Printer for Scotland. P98 Step Up 3D review from www.totalfilm.com. Reprinted with permission of Future Publishing. P98 Worldpop.com review from www.westlife.org. Reprinted with kind permission. P100 'Twilight' book review by Stephenie Meyer. Reprinted with permission.

The publisher would like to thank the following for their kind permission to reproduce their photographs:

Piv-v FLPA Images of Nature: SA TEAM / FN / Minden; Pvi-vii FLPA Images of Nature: SA TEAM / FN / Minden; Piii FLPA Images of Nature: SA TEAM / FN / Minden; P6 Getty Images: Peter Dazeley; P14 iStockphoto: Andrew Howe; P17 Rex Features: c.ABC Inc / Reverett; P25 Getty Images: Digital Vision; P32 iStockphoto: David Gomez; P40 Photolibrary.com: Brian Mitchell; P41 Photolibrary.com: Brian Mitchell; P48-49 FLPA Images of Nature: SA TEAM / FN / Minden; P52 Alamy Images: Blend Images; P60 Getty Images; P70 iStockphoto: Catherine Yeulet; P77 Getty Images: Bob Thomas Sports Photography; P85 Alamy Images: imagegallery; P92 Alamy Images: Inspirestock Inc.

All other images © Pearson Education Limited

Every effort has been made to contact copyright holders of material reproduced in this book. Any omissions will be rectified in subsequent printings if notice is given to the publishers.

Contents

Introduction

This Workbook is designed to help you focus your revision and improve your grade in WJEC GCSE English and English Language.

Some students think that there is no need to revise for English and English Language. This is simply not true! You can do things to improve your chances of getting a good grade and you can revise for English and English Language as much as for any of your other subjects.

The more you revise and practise past paper questions, the more confident you will become in knowing just what the examiner is looking for. By making yourself familiar with the type of questions being asked and the mark schemes used by the examiners, you will be increasing your chances of getting a higher grade.

How to improve your revision techniques

1 The first thing to do is to make use of your own teacher, as they are a very valuable resource! Listen carefully to all the revision tips your teacher gives you in lesson time. If there is something you are unsure about, remember to ask. Your teacher may hold extra revision classes at lunchtime in the run-up to the exam sessions. If so, make sure you take advantage of this opportunity.

2 Check that you are familiar with what the exam papers look like, how many marks are awarded for each question and how much you will be expected to write in your answer booklet.

3 When you are ready to revise, find a quiet area away from any distractions like noise or television. Remember to take regular breaks and pace yourself. It is difficult to concentrate for very long periods of time. Breaking your revision into manageable sessions is much more worthwhile and you will remember more in the long run.

4 Use a checklist like the one on the opposite page. This could be a useful starting point for you to work out exactly what you know already, and to help you find any gaps in your knowledge.

5 The most effective way to revise is through active strategies. This means:
   - practising the skills you have studied
   - taking part in completing revision activities
   - comparing your answers with sample answers to see where you can improve your performance.

6 When you practise answering past paper questions, always time yourself. This will help you to understand what it will feel like to be under pressure when you are writing in the exam itself.

7 Finally, be positive: think about what you *can* do, not what you can't. Good luck!

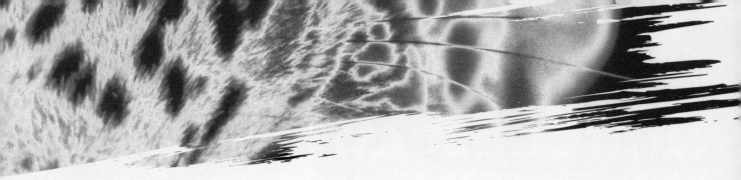

Revision checklist

How confident do you feel about each of the areas below that you need to revise for your exam?

Fill in the revision checklist below.

- Tick green if you feel confident about this topic.
- Tick amber if you know some things, but revision will help to make your knowledge and skills the best they can be.
- Tick red if you are not confident about two or more aspects of this topic.

There will be a chance to fill in this table after your revision and before your exam, to see how much progress you have made during your revision.

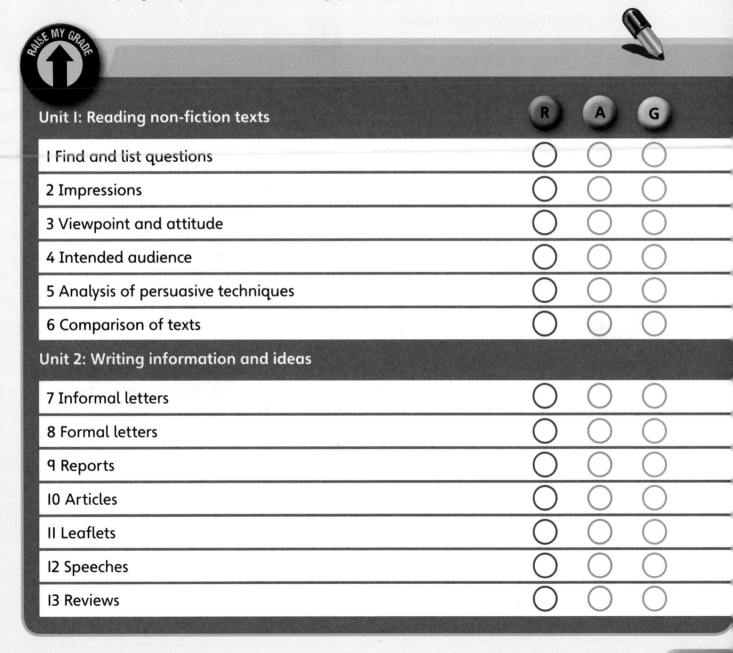

Unit I: Reading non-fiction texts	R	A	G
I Find and list questions	○	○	○
2 Impressions	○	○	○
3 Viewpoint and attitude	○	○	○
4 Intended audience	○	○	○
5 Analysis of persuasive techniques	○	○	○
6 Comparison of texts	○	○	○
Unit 2: Writing information and ideas			
7 Informal letters	○	○	○
8 Formal letters	○	○	○
9 Reports	○	○	○
10 Articles	○	○	○
II Leaflets	○	○	○
12 Speeches	○	○	○
13 Reviews	○	○	○

Using the WJEC GCSE English and English Language Revision Workbook

The WJEC GCSE English and English Language Student Workbook has been written to help you to revise the skills and knowledge that you will have covered in your GCSE English/English Language course over Year 10 and Year 11.

The Workbook has been designed for you to revise **actively**. There is room for you to write answers to activities and practise exam questions, though in some cases you will need to continue your answer on a separate sheet of paper. The **'Extra paper'** icon will indicate where this is necessary. You are encouraged to highlight and annotate exam questions and texts as you will in the exam.

Every lesson will open with the **'Skills to raise my grade'** table. You need to decide how confident you are with each of the skills listed. You can record your confidence using a traffic-light system. The lesson then goes over these skills and at the end of the lesson you review your confidence. Hopefully your knowledge of the skills will have improved.

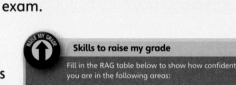

Skills to raise my grade

Fill in the RAG table below to show how confident you are in the following areas:

	R	A	G
I can read and understand questions that are asking me to find information in a text.	O	O	O
I can use a range of reading skills to find information in a text.	O	O	O
I can select the correct information to answer the question.	O	O	O
I can include enough information in my answer to score full marks.	O	O	O

Each activity suggests how much time you should spend on it. This is for guidance only. Where an activity involves answering an exam question, the timings will be linked to how much time you will have to answer this type of question in the exam itself.

10 minutes

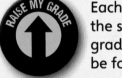

Each lesson has a **'Raise my grade'** activity. In these activities you will practise the specific skills that you have revised in the lesson, and try to improve a lower grade answer by one grade. This is the Foundation Tier Workbook, so you will be focusing on grades F–C.

At the end of each lesson there is a **'GradeStudio'** section. This is to give you an opportunity to read examiner comments and mark schemes, and to match these to sample student answers. This exam work should help you understand the mark scheme and how to get the highest grade you are capable of.

GradeStudio

15 minutes

Read this extract from the article 'Piling up Problems'. Then read the student responses to the that follows it.

You can find answers to the Workbook activities online at www.pearsonschools.co.uk/gcse2010/wjecenglish Click on Free Resources and open the Foundation answer file.

Good luck with your revision. Remember – you still have time to improve your performance in the exam by at least a grade.

In the exam room, remember to be confident, take a deep breath and don't panic! Read all the questions carefully and put into practice all the advice from your teacher and the helpful hints you will find in this Workbook.

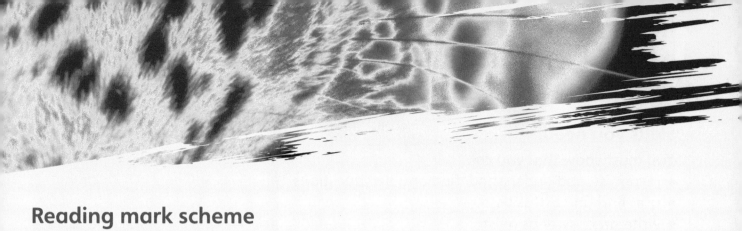

Reading mark scheme
Grade descriptions

C grade answer

(8–10 marks)

- Selects appropriate detail from the text
- Shows understanding of the key areas in the text
- The answer will have a clear understanding of the question

D grade answer

(6–7 marks)

- Makes simple comments about the text
- Some focus on the question
- Will include some appropriate detail from the text

E grade answer

(5 marks)

- Simple comments based on surface features of the text
- Some awareness of the writer's arguments or ideas
- Some selection of details from the text

F grade answer

(3–4 marks)

- Short answers which may be lacking in focus
- A few details from the text may be used in the answer

G grade answer

(2–3 marks)

- Very short, brief answers
- Little development of any ideas
- May not link ideas to the text

Find and list questions

Skills you need:

You must show that you can:
- recognise and understand 'find and list' questions
- use 'find and list' skills
- write an answer as a list

Skills to raise my grade

RAISE MY GRADE

Fill in the RAG table below to show how confident you are in the following areas:

	R	A	G
I can read and understand questions that are asking me to find information in a text.	○	○	○
I can use a range of reading skills to find information in a text.	○	○	○
I can select the correct information to answer the question.	○	○	○
I can include enough information in my answer to score full marks.	○	○	○

Questions that ask you to 'find and list' information are usually good opportunities to score marks quickly in the exam, but this will only work if you follow the instructions closely and read the material carefully.

Activity 1

4 minutes

1. In order to check that you are confident about what find and list questions are asking you to do, read these questions carefully and tick the ones where you think you are being asked to list or find information.

		✓ or ✗
I	List ten activities mentioned or shown in the brochure.	
2	How does the writer persuade readers to become blood donors?	
3	Make a list of what is making children unhealthy, according to the article.	
4	How does the factsheet try to get its message across effectively?	
5	What equipment is given to you when you play paintball?	

2. Now highlight the word in each question which suggests it is a list or find question.

Top tips! Find and list questions

1 Always read the question carefully. Underline key words so you know exactly what information to look for.

2 If the question asks you to list or write down, that is exactly what you must do. You don't need to write in full sentences.

3 Make sure you are looking at the correct part of the text – you will not score any marks for information taken from the wrong section.

4 Work your way through the text, line by line, so you don't miss out vital information. Underline or highlight each point you make as you go along.

5 Check that you have found the correct number of points asked for in the question. If the question asks for ten points and you write down six, you will not score full marks.

6 If you are asked for ten points, it is worth finding an extra one or two in case you have made any mistakes.

7 Only spend a maximum of 12 minutes on questions like these.

Activity 2

10 minutes

Read the leaflet for Bristol Zoo Gardens on page 4 and the following exam question.

List ten things that you can do at Bristol Zoo Gardens.   *(10 marks)*

1 Highlight the key words in the exam question, then work through the text line by line and underline each point you find.

2 Now write your answer.

Welcome to Bristol Zoo Gardens

Enjoy an amazing world of animals, all within our spectacular, award-winning, 12-acre gardens. With over 450 species – including nine animal houses under cover – you can enjoy your visit, whatever the weather.

Protecting wildlife

When you visit Bristol Zoo, you're also helping to conserve and protect endangered species and habitats. Our admission prices include a 10% voluntary donation, which we use to support our conservation projects.

Get involved

There are so many ways that you can help protect wildlife, so why not:
- become an annual member
- become a keeper for the day
- buy an animal adoption as a unique gift
- make a donation to our Conservation Fund

What will you see next time?

Bristol Zoo Gardens
www.bristolzoo.org.uk

Bristol Zoo Gardens

Coral Café
Feeling peckish? Pop into our underwater themed Coral Café for a tasty snack, homemade lunchtime specials and hot and cold drinks.

Amazing Animals shows
Experience our amazing shows, which include free-flying birds of prey, Colin the red-ruffed lemur or Archie the armadillo.

Explorers' Creek
With three exciting areas, you can splash in the water play area, brave the wobbly bridge in the Forest of Birds and feed nectar to colourful parrots at Feed the Lorikeets (*small charge for nectar, subject to availability*).

ZooRopia
Come and experience ZooRopia, Bristol Zoo's aerial adventure for everyone aged five and up. Swing next to some of our most popular apes, fly down the zip wire and enjoy fantastic views over the Zoo (*restrictions and charges apply, subject to availability*).

Walk-through exhibits
Get up close to the animals in our exciting, immersive exhibits including Feed the Lorikeets, Lemur walk-through, Seal & Penguin Coasts and Butterfly Forest.

Animal Encounters
Take the opportunity to meet some of our smaller animals close-up.

Keeper talks
11:00 – Lion talk
12:30 – Gorilla feeding and talk
13:30 – Butterfly talk
14:30 – Lemur talk
15:00 – Penguin feeding and talk
15:30 – Seal feeding and talk

Sometimes you will be asked to find **specific details** in the text. For these questions you will need to work through the material in the same way as for listing questions.

The texts are usually leaflets and brochures and there are often several parts to the question. Make sure that you answer **all** parts of the question, otherwise you will lose marks. Here is an example of an exam question for you to practise this skill.

Activity 3

10 minutes

Read the leaflet entitled 'What a Waste!' on page 6, then answer the questions below. Look carefully at the number of marks for each question when you are giving your answer.

1 What percentage of waste is recycled in Mid Sussex? *(1 mark)*

2 What percentage of the food we buy in the UK is thrown away? *(1 mark)*

3 Give three examples of the main reasons why food is thrown away. *(3 marks)*

4 Give three examples of unavoidable food waste that could be composted. *(3 marks)*

5 Explain the difference between 'Use by' and 'Best before' dates on food. *(2 marks)*

MID SUSSEX
DISTRICT COUNCIL

RECYCLE
for a better Mid Sussex

WHAT A WASTE!

We already recycle 40% of our waste in Mid Sussex, but around 30% of what is left is food.

Most of this is, or once was, perfectly good food.

Throwing away good food is a terrible waste. In the UK we throw away about 30% of all the food we buy. That's one shopping bag out of every three!

The main reasons for this are:

- Too much was prepared.
- We don't use up 'leftovers'.
- We forgot what was in the cupboard and missed its 'Use-by' date.

Some food waste is made of things like peelings and cores, but the majority is, or once was, perfectly good food. If we planned, stored and managed our food better, we could reduce our food waste and save ourselves money.

On average, UK households spend £420 a year on food that they then throw away. For example, each day 1.3 million unopened yoghurts, 5,500 whole chickens and 440,000 ready-meals are thrown away in the UK. Add to this the cost for local authorities to send this waste to huge rubbish dumps and the total cost is high.

Food waste sent to rubbish dumps generates methane, a greenhouse gas far more powerful than carbon dioxide. Methane increases the problem of global warming. Eliminating this waste would have the same impact on carbon emissions as taking 1 in 5 cars off UK roads.

HOME COMPOSTING

Home composting is a great way to prevent unavoidable food waste such as peelings, cores, eggshells and teabags ending up in rubbish dumps, and can do wonders for the garden.

DATE LABELS EXPLAINED

Use-by	Best before
'Use-by' dates are usually found on chilled products such as cooked meats, soft cheeses and dairy-based desserts. In terms of safety, never eat products after this date, and observe storage instructions.	'Best before' dates are usually on longer shelf-life foods such as frozen, tinned or dried goods, and refer to qualify rather than safety. It should be safe to eat food after the 'best before' date, but food may no longer be at its best.

Storage of food waste

Once in your landfill bin, food waste will start to rot and may cause unpleasant odours. Reducing this waste will not only save you money and slim your bin, but will also make your landfill waste less offensive.

For further information please look at our website: www.midsussex.gov.uk

Activity 4

10 minutes

Read these two responses to the exam questions you answered in Activity 3, and look at the examiner comments.

Student 1

Question 1 has been misread and gives the answer for wastage in the UK, not Mid Sussex.

Question 2 has also been misread and gives the answer for wastage in Mid Sussex, not the UK.

1 30% ✗

2 40% ✗

3 Forgetting to freeze it. ✓

Question 3 is worth 3 marks but the answer only finds one point.

4 Use by means never eat food after the date. ✓

5 Keep them in the fridge. ✓

Question 4 only answers the first part of the question.

Question 5 again only finds one point instead of three.

Examiner comments

Grade F answer (4 marks)

Student 2

This candidate clearly knows what to do in this type of question and has read the leaflet and questions very carefully.

All parts of the questions have been answered, so marks haven't been thrown away carelessly. There are no mistakes and every answer is clear – in fact, to make sure that full marks are scored, an extra point has been made on question 3 as a safety net.

1 40% ✓

2 30% ✓

3 Forgetting to freeze food, ✓ too much food prepared, ✓ missing use-by dates, ✓ forgetting what there is in the cupboard already. (✓)

4 Use by means never eat the food after the date. ✓ Best before means the food should be safe to eat but it may not be at its best. ✓

5 Keep them in the fridge, ✓ buy fresh fruit and veg twice a week, ✓ don't buy it in bulk. ✓

Examiner comments

Grade C answer (10 marks)

1 Compare these two answers with your own response. What were the strengths of your answer and how could you improve it?

Read this extract from the article 'Piling up Problems'. Then read the student responses to the exam question that follows it.

Piling up problems

Children as young as eight are showing signs of heart disease, say health experts.

They blame junk food and couch potato lifestyles, and warn that a generation of youngsters is risking obesity, sickness and an early death.

A campaign to highlight the dangers was launched yesterday at the Science Museum in London.

Organisers revealed that the average child will consume 52 stones of saturated fat between the ages of six and sixteen – the equivalent of 1,314 packets of lard. That is about 80lb, or 14 packs, too much.

While obesity used to be a problem only for adults, the experts say it now affects increasing numbers of British children.

One in five is overweight. And the earlier they become so, the greater the risk of fat-related disease in later life.

The museum based its findings on a survey of 4,500 children visiting its Science of Sport Exhibition.

Almost all of them knew the message about exercise and healthy eating, including which foods were good and which bad. But few appeared to have taken any notice.

More than 90 per cent of the boys said playing computer games, not sport, was their favourite activity outside school. Almost half the girls said they took part in sport only once a week or even less often.

Just under half the children said they preferred watching sport to taking part.

About 45 per cent had been on a diet at some time, nearly a quarter skipped breakfast, and almost half ate fruit and vegetables less than once a day.

Only 35 per cent walked or cycled to school.

Research at London hospitals has discovered that a disturbing number of youngsters aged eight and nine have high cholesterol levels – an indicator of possible heart problems.

Last year, doctors also found that one sixteen-year-old in three was showing early signs of heart disease.

According to the article, what are the dangers for youngsters of an unhealthy lifestyle? **(5 marks)**

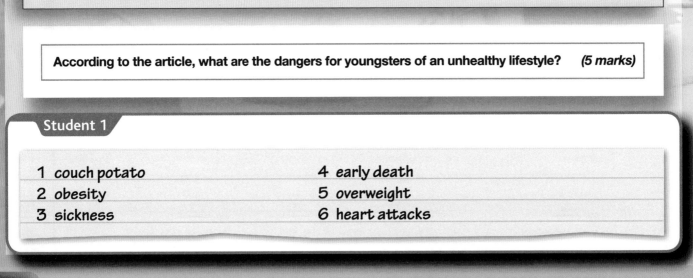

Student 1

1 couch potato
2 obesity
3 sickness
4 early death
5 overweight
6 heart attacks

The dangers of an unhealthy lifestyle for youngsters is if they eat too much junk food they will become lazy, and I think this is silly because they should be outside running around and playing football. If they smoke they might end up looking older than they are and they might have heart attacks. They should eat more fruit.

1 Which of these two answers would score the higher mark? Give **two** reasons to explain your choice.

_____

_____

_____

2 Using the grade descriptions on page vii, what grade do you think each answer would receive? ☐ ☐

3 Based on all the information in this section about find and list questions, write a list of **five** important things you need to do to make sure you score full marks on questions like these.

_____

_____

_____

_____

_____

Skills to raise my grade

Now that you have completed this lesson on find and list questions, it's time to fill in the RAG table below to see if your confidence has improved.

R   A   G

	R	A	G
I can read and understand questions that are asking me to find information in a text.	○	○	○
I can use a range of reading skills to find information in a text.	○	○	○
I can select the correct information to answer the question.	○	○	○
I can include enough information in my answer to score full marks.	○	○	○

2 Impressions

Skills you need:
You must show that you can:
- recognise and understand 'impressions' questions
- write about the kind of view you have of a place, person or organisation from what the author says
- organise your material carefully and find evidence to support your impressions

Skills to raise my grade

Fill in the RAG table below to show how confident you are in the following areas:

	R	A	G
I can recognise an impressions question.	○	○	○
I can understand how a view of a person, place or organisation is created from what is written about them.	○	○	○
I can organise my material and write my answer in a clear and straightforward way.	○	○	○
I can use evidence from the text to support my points.	○	○	○

In the exam you might be asked a question about what impression an article or factsheet gives about an individual, a place or an organisation.

When answering questions about impressions, you should consider the following points.
- Impressions are simply the views/ideas you have about a place, person or organisation after reading about them.
- These views/impressions are created by the words/phrases used by the author.

Activity 1

3 minutes

Look at the list of describing words below.

Sort them into two columns: one for the words creating a negative impression and the other for words creating a positive impression. The first one has been done for you in the table opposite.

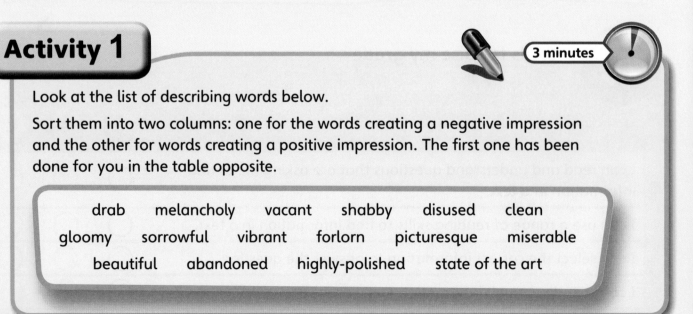

> drab   melancholy   vacant   shabby   disused   clean
> gloomy   sorrowful   vibrant   forlorn   picturesque   miserable
> beautiful   abandoned   highly-polished   state of the art

Positive	Negative
beautiful	drab

Top tips! Impressions questions

1 When answering questions like this, always underline the key words in the question to make sure you know exactly what to do.
2 Check that you are focusing on the correct section of the text.
3 Remember you should always look for a range of different impressions, probably about five or six.
4 You need to support each of your impressions with words/phrases from the text.
5 As you do for all questions, work your way through the text, line by line, so you don't miss out vital information. Underline or highlight each point you make as you go along.

RAISE MY GRADE

Activity 2

20 minutes

You are going to read an advertisement on page 12 from the environmental charity, Friends of the Earth. The advert is reporting about how ruthless timber cutters take advantage of innocent Amazonian Indians for their mahogany trees.

1 Look at this exam question based on the advertisement and underline the key words within it.

What impressions do we have of the timber cutters? How does the advertisement create this impression? *(10 marks)*

2 Next, read the extract carefully, underlining or highlighting any points you find that could help you answer the exam question.

PLEASE WILL YOU STOP PAYING TO HAVE MY PEOPLE MURDERED?

There was only one possible name for Friends of the Earth's report on the Amazonian mahogany trade: 'Mahogany is Murder'. What follows has been pieced together from the evidence of many different Indians.

Let me tell you how it is with us Indians, and the mahogany cutters. On March 28th, 1988, about 100 Indians met in a house by a river, to discuss what to do about the timber thieves who were cutting and stealing mahogany trees from their lands.

A boat came up the river. It was the timber cutter, Oscar Branco, with 16 hired gunmen. The men got out and shouted that they had come to kill everyone. They started firing.

The Indians tried to flee in canoes, but many were gunned down. Fourteen Indians, including children, were killed. Twenty two more were wounded.

Everyone knew who the killers were. Branco was named as the ringleader by Brazil's Chief of Federal Police. Eleven of the sixteen gunmen have been identified. Yet four years have passed and not one has been prosecuted. Those Indians and their children – their deaths didn't count.

The Indian lands are ours by right forever. No outsider is meant to come into them without our permission. But they do come, the timber cutters. They come because the mahogany is so precious.

They try all kinds of tricks to get us to part with the timber. Men came in trucks to some Indian villages. They gave out radios, torches, T-shirts, biscuits and tins of food. The villagers were very grateful for these gifts. Some weeks later the men returned. They said that the goods had been given on credit and they had come to collect payment – in trees.

Some Indians have been fooled into agreeing to contacts which are not at all to their benefit. Two young Xikrin Indians, who had no authority to speak for their tribe, were persuaded to sign a deal with a big timber company, one of those companies which supplies your British importers.

The deal said that half the wood taken from the forest would be granted free to the company over the cost of cutting the trees. The rest of the trees, worth about £300 each, were to be bought from the Xikrin Indians for £10 each. But when the final settlement came the Indians got no money, only a bill claiming that they owed the timber company £6000 for 'merchandise'.

It is when we Indians resist the invasion of our lands that the killing starts. During an argument, a tree cutter threw an Indian woman's baby into a river where it drowned. Even if the timber cutters will not murder us with guns, they have other ways to kill our people.

The mahogany trees grow apart so the timber cutters hack roads through the forest to reach them. Nearly half of our people have died from diseases brought by the timber cutters since first contact with the outside world.

While our people die, the forest disappears forever. It is greed that is killing us, and the trees and the animals. Your greed for mahogany. You in Britain buy more than half the mahogany Brazil produces. Look! That deep red glow in your mahogany dinner table is the blood of murdered Indians. Listen! The clatter of your mahogany lavatory seat is the gunfire that killed Indian children. You must do all you can to help those who are fighting to end this evil trade.

Friends of the Earth campaigns locally, nationally, internationally and tirelessly against the timber trade which is accelerating the demise of the Earth's last rainforests and their peoples. Since our campaign began, British imports of tropical timber have dropped by a third. But we need to do so much more. Time is running out. People are dying. The forest is vanishing. Please join us. Please do it now.

FRIENDS *of the*
earth
for the planet for people

3 Complete the table below to focus your reading and organise your material.

What impressions do we get of the timber cutters?	What details from the advertisement give us this impression?
Ruthless	'16 hired gunmen' 'they shouted that they had come to kill everyone'
Cunning	

4 Write your answer to this question using full sentences and paragraphs in the space below. It is a good idea to begin your answer by using the words of the question. For example:

12 minutes

My first impression of the timber cutters is …

_____

_____

_____

_____

_____

_____

_____

_____

_____

_____

_____

_____

Read the leaflet 'The Effects of a Pack of 20 on an Expectant Mother' and the exam question below.

> **What impression of fox hunting do we have from this leaflet? How are these impressions created?**
> *(10 marks)*

THE EFFECTS OF A PACK OF 20 ON AN EXPECTANT MOTHER

It's a disgusting habit. But one that fox hunters seem loath to give up. In an average year, they get through around 20,000 cubs, dog-foxes and vixens. Even heavily pregnant vixens are considered fair game.

Selective with the truth, some fox hunters maintain there is no cruelty. Post-mortem examinations of foxes savaged by hounds prove otherwise. Typical findings include, 'Extensive wounds to abdomen and thorax', 'intestines hanging out' and 'death caused by pathological shock'. A 'quick nip to the neck' it isn't.

Foxes that manage to go to ground during a hunt face a terrifying and protracted ordeal. Escape routes are blocked and terriers sent in to corner their prey. The ensuing underground battle is nasty and brutish.

It is not short. The fox may well die underground fighting for its life. (The terriers also sustain injuries.) If it's still alive the hunters' digging will expose it. The best the poor creature can hope for now is a gunshot.

Those animals that escape the hunt don't necessarily escape the suffering. The stress and exertion of the chase is traumatic beyond imagination. This, the fox hunters insist, is sport.

71% of the British people disagree. They think hunting with dogs should be banned (MORI). Don't be passive. Please write to your MP. Ensure that on 28 November he or she supports Michael Foster's Private Member's Bill to ban hunting with dogs.

IFAW.org
INTERNATIONAL FUND FOR ANIMAL WELFARE
A Better World for Animals and People

Make sure your MP opposes hunting with dogs on November 28th.
For more information call IFAW on 0800 01 02 03.

1 Write your answer to the exam question in the space provided below.

_____

_____

_____

_____

_____

_____

_____

_____

2 Using the grade descriptions on page vii, and the success criteria table below, try to work out a mark and a grade for your answer.

	✓ or ✗
Did you underline the key words in the question?	
Did you highlight words/phrases as you read the leaflet?	
Did you find at least five impressions?	
Did you find details from the leaflet to support your points?	
Did you include any words/phrases you find to support your impressions?	

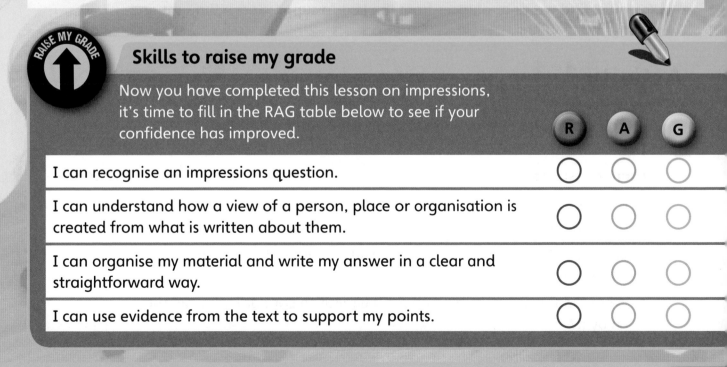

RAISE MY GRADE

Skills to raise my grade

Now you have completed this lesson on impressions, it's time to fill in the RAG table below to see if your confidence has improved.

	R	A	G
I can recognise an impressions question.	○	○	○
I can understand how a view of a person, place or organisation is created from what is written about them.	○	○	○
I can organise my material and write my answer in a clear and straightforward way.	○	○	○
I can use evidence from the text to support my points.	○	○	○

3 Viewpoint and attitude

Skills you need:

You must show that you can:
- recognise a 'viewpoint and attitude' (thoughts and feelings) question
- organise material and find evidence to support points when answering a 'viewpoint and attitude' question

Skills to raise my grade

Fill in the RAG table below to show how confident you are in the following areas:

	R	A	G
I can recognise a viewpoint and attitude (thoughts and feelings) question.	○	○	○
I can work through the text methodically (line by line) when reading.	○	○	○
I can organise and write my material in a clear and straightforward way.	○	○	○
I can include evidence from the text to support my points.	○	○	○

When answering a question about viewpoint and attitude, you should always remember the following points.
- 'Viewpoint and attitude' means exactly the same thing as 'thoughts and feelings', so don't be put off by the wording of the question.
- Work through the piece of text you have been given line by line, so you can track the thoughts and feelings of the writer as they change and develop.
- You must find words or phrases from the text to support each thought and feeling that you find.

Activity 1

3 minutes

Tick the exam questions that are asking you to write about the opinions of the author.

Exam questions	✓ or X
1 How does the leaflet try to persuade you to visit Warwick Castle?	
2 Compare what the two texts say about Sheffield.	
3 What are the writer's thoughts and feelings about the PGL holiday his children went on?	
4 What did the children enjoy about their visit to London? Why did they enjoy it?	

Top tips! Viewpoint and attitude questions

1 Always read the question carefully. Underline the key words so you know exactly what to do.
2 Make sure that you are focusing on the correct area of the text.
3 Work your way through the text, line by line, so you don't miss out vital information. Underline or highlight the thoughts and feelings when you find them.
4 Use the wording of the question to help you keep your focus in your answer. Try to begin your sentences with 'The author feels...' or 'The writer thinks...'
5 Avoid using the phrases 'I think that...' or 'I feel that...' because this will encourage you to give your own opinion and you will not score any marks.

Activity 2

20 minutes

Read this article written by Mecca Ibrahim.

Why we all hate Jamie Oliver

– by Mecca Ibrahim

Obviously we don't all hate him, just about 90% of the UK population hate him. The 10% of the population who like Jamie Oliver includes Jamie's family, his sponsors – Sainsbury's – and the barking mad people who have bought his cookery book in the past and will doubtless buy his new book *Jamie's Kitchen* too (sadly these people amount to millions).

Who is Jamie Oliver? Well, if you live in the USA there is a fair chance you haven't heard of him. If you live in the UK and you have a TV, you will see this cockney 'chef' appearing on countless adverts for Sainsbury's supermarket as well as in his programmes. Jamie has this great ability to cause emotions in people. Love him or hate him, you can't really be indifferent to him. My husband liked his first TV series and really liked his second TV series. By the third series we both wanted to throw the trusty food mixer at the TV.

From a refreshingly different TV chef who was a bit overcome by his own success, Jamie became self-centred and self-important. There are many things I hate about Jamie: his vast apartment with a basketball hoop in it, the way he slides down the banister like the overgrown kid he is, his scooter, the way he is best buddies with the people in his local shops, and the fact that he earns millions. But the worst thing of all is his terrible accent. Despite being brought up in Cambridge (absolutely nowhere near London), he persists in trying to sound as if he is A True Cockney. So to hear some buffoon making loads of money by saying 'Pukka', 'Lovely Jubbly', 'Alrwroigt' and 'Darlink' is ever so slightly annoying.

And what's this about his new restaurant called 'Fifteen'? Jamie takes some unemployed street urchins and tries to turn them into first class chefs and then puts the whole thing on TV. Now having seen most episodes of *Jamie's Kitchen*, I still think Mr Oliver may have bitten off more than he can chew. The kids from London were really raw, knew nothing about

food, were surly and even from episode one you could see they had attitude problems. Jamie mortgaged his house to come up with money for the restaurant, but I honestly don't see why you would risk your house – if not for a publicity stunt.

For most of the series Jamie looked downcast (not much was 'pukka') and rather like one of the kids himself. This was particularly so when the college tutors were telling him about his prized fifteen recruits playing truant and not paying attention in class.

Anyway my rant is done. I am sure Jamie is a fine cook. His food looks good so perhaps that's all that matters and if he's got 'geezers', 'blokes' and ordinary men thinking that cookery is trendy that's only to be encouraged too.

Anyway, good luck to you, Jamie.

Viewpoint and attitude

1 Look at the following exam question and underline the key words.

> **What are the writer's attitudes to Jamie Oliver? How does she make these attitudes clear? You should consider:**
> * **what she says about Jamie Oliver**
> * **her choice of words and phrases**
> * **other ways she makes it clear what she thinks about him.**   *(10 marks)*

2 How many paragraphs should you include in your answer?
Look at the bullet points in the question.

_____

3 Complete the table below and find some of your own points to help you organise your material before you start writing your answer.

Remember that in the actual exam, you could quickly draw a table of your own to help you sort out your ideas and evidence in a clear and straightforward way.

The writer's attitude towards Jamie Oliver	Evidence
She hates him	
She thinks he's full of himself	
	'Many things I hate about Jamie … the fact that he earns millions'
She admires his cookery skills and praises the way he has changed men's attitude to cookery	

How does she make these attitudes clear?	Evidence
She makes fun of his expressions	
	She wanted to destroy her TV set when he was on

4 Using all the information you have gathered, write your answer to the question in full sentences and paragraphs in the space below.

_____

_____

_____

_____

_____

_____

_____

_____

_____

_____

_____

_____

_____

_____

_____

Activity 3

10 minutes

You can now assess your answer and grade your work.

1 Answer the questions below, thinking about your answer to Activity 2.

	✓ or ✗	How would you improve on this next time? (For example, include more evidence.)
Did you work through the text methodically, line by line?		
Did you find different thoughts and feelings as you tracked through?		
Did you find examples of words/phrases used by the author to support your points?		

2 Using the grade descriptions on page vii to help you, try to grade your answer.

My answer is a grade _____ because

_____

_____

_____

_____

_____

_____

_____

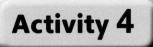

Activity 4

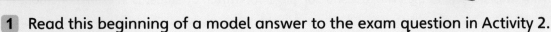

10 minutes

1 Read this beginning of a model answer to the exam question in Activity 2.

C grade answer

It is clear from the title and the very first sentence that the writer hates Jamie Oliver. She says, '90% of the UK population hate him' and suggests the only people who don't actually hate him are those like his family or sponsors. This exaggeration of the percentage that hate him is continued when she tells us she is so tired of seeing him on TV that she wanted to 'throw the trusty food mixer at the TV'. She suggests that in the UK it's almost impossible to switch on the TV without seeing him because he's 'on countless adverts ... as well as his own food programmes'...

2 This is an example of a good response that will score a grade C if the answer continues in this way. Can you think of two strengths in this answer?

3 Highlight the points made in one colour and highlight the evidence used to support the points in a different colour to see how effectively it has been done in the answer. Put a tick above every sentence that scores a mark.

4 Using the tips you have picked up so far, finish writing the rest of the answer in the space below.

1 Read the following two answers to the exam question on page 18, written by students in exam conditions.

Student 1

The title states that we 'all hate' Jamie Oliver although this is to attract the reader. Mecca is very critical of his book by saying that the people who bought it are 'barking mad'. She clearly has no care for Jamie by stating that when she saw him on television she wanted to 'throw the trusty food mixer at the TV'. She feels that Jamie Oliver is concerned about himself by describing him as 'self-centred'. Mecca is giving the impression of not wanting to be anywhere near by stating that Cambridge is nowhere near London. She doesn't also agree with him risking his money by saying it is a 'publicity stunt'. We are given the thought that the writer may have a certain amount of jealousy.

Student 2

The writer of 'Why we all hate Jamie Oliver' by Mecca Ibrahim clearly shows her thoughts and feelings about Jamie Oliver. She begins with how much the population of the UK hate him and the percentage who do like him are his friends, family and sponsors. She writes it in a very sarcastic way to get her point across: 'Just about 90% of the UK population hate him'. She also seems very jealous of Jamie Oliver. She writes about his apartment and how he acts like an 'overgrown kid'. She also makes him out to be a fake, by saying where he lives and how he speaks. He was brought up in Cambridge, also saying 'absolutely nowhere near London' in a very sarcastic and nasty way, which shows how annoyed she gets with him. She also points out that he is trying to sound like a 'true cockney' but he isn't, which shows that she hates Jamie Oliver with a passion. She also thinks that the restaurant called 'Fifteen' is a publicity stunt and this shows how jealous she is of him by making him look bad when really he is trying to help out some jobless teenagers with their life.

Student 3

I think personally the writer makes it clear she is blatantly jealous of the man. It's probably one of the most immature letters I've read. The reason for this is she claims to hate him because of his house, the money he earns, his TV programme and his accent. She also attempts to mock his idea for 'Fifteen' and taking in unemployed street urchins. Personally, I think that's a great idea as the less people unemployed walking the streets the better. I don't think she has the right to judge him personally. She also uses the word 'hate' to describe what she feels about him. As she doesn't know him, she has no reason to hate him. It's just jealousy.

2 Using the grade descriptions given on page vii to help you, can you match the following marks, grades and examiner comments to the correct student answers? Fill in the table below with your answers and explain your choices.

Comment 1

5 marks = Grade E
This response loses sight of the question and the student gives his/her own opinion which doesn't score any marks. The response does show simple awareness of attitude and even technique but lacks a methodical approach.

Comment 2

8 marks = Grade C
The answer makes a number of points and offers a few comments and supports them. The answer drifts away from the question a little at the end and into opinion.

Comment 3

5/6 marks = Grade E/D
This answer makes a few sensible comments but it is limited. Comments are linked to textual evidence but it misses so many points.

Student answer	Grade	Reason for choosing this grade
1		
2		
3		

RAISE MY GRADE

Skills to raise my grade

Now you have completed this lesson on viewpoint and attitude, it's time to fill in the RAG table below to see if your confidence has improved.

	R	A	G
I can recognise a viewpoint and attitude (thoughts and feelings) question.	○	○	○
I can work through the text methodically (line by line) when reading.	○	○	○
I can organise and write my material in a clear and straightforward way.	○	○	○
I can include words from the text to support my points.	○	○	○

Skills you need:

You must show that you can:
- recognise a question asking whom a text is aimed at
- understand how a text is aimed at a particular audience

Skills to raise my grade

Fill in the RAG table below to show how confident you are in the following areas:

	R	A	G
I can recognise a question asking me whom the text is aimed at.	○	○	○
I can understand how to work out the intended audience of a text.	○	○	○
I can organise my answers in a clear and straightforward way.	○	○	○
I can use words and details from the text to support my points.	○	○	○

Activity 1

4 minutes

When companies advertise a new product to sell, they have a specific and intended audience (sometimes called a target audience) in mind.

This means the product would be aimed at a particular range of people, usually because of their age, gender or interests.

1 Try to match up the following products with their intended audiences/target groups. Choose from the intended audiences in the box on the right.

> Children
> Teenagers
> Adults
> Old people
> Car owners

Product	Intended audience
New flavour of bubble gum	
Stairlift	
Car insurance	
Washing powder	
Mobile phone	

Top tips! Intended audience questions

1 Questions that ask 'Who is this text aimed at?' are usually linked to advertisements.

2 You need to work out the intended audience by looking at what the advertisement/ leaflet says and the language used.

3 Pictures are also very important in helping you decide on the intended audience. Think about whether there are pictures of children/families/older people and so on.

Activity 2

20 minutes

Read the following article entitled 'Your weight and BMI', then answer the questions that follow it on page 26.

Healthy Eating

Your weight and BMI
Healthy or not?

Healthy eating has been a hot topic for some time. But more recently, the issue of obesity has been grabbing the headlines. This is because obesity is becoming more common, and is a problem for many people, especially young people right now.

To put you in the picture, obesity is a medical term that means someone's weight is likely to cause serious health problems in the future. Some of these problems could be cancer, heart disease, diabetes and depression.

Sometimes it can be difficult to know if you've got a weight problem or not. Your clothes might fit you fine and you feel like you eat pretty healthily – after all, you don't pig out on crisps, canned drinks and chocolate all day. Or do you? Maybe you look at all the other people out there who are bigger and heavier than you and perhaps you don't feel like it's an issue for you.

Or maybe you know that you're bigger than you'd like to be. You can see that your clothes don't fit as well as you'd like them to, and OK, not everyone can look like (or wants to look like!) a Pussy Cat Doll, or David Beckham, but you know you could look and feel better.

Perhaps you don't doubt you've got a problem, but you don't know where to start!

The best place for anyone to start is with the BMI index chart.

This can tell you whether you are a healthy weight for your age and height. Once you know this, you can work out whether you want to do something about it or not. And even if you come out smelling of strawberries, within the right range, let's face it – most of us could do with being a bit healthier. There are far more benefits to a good diet than just being a healthy weight.

1 Do you think this article is aimed at teenagers or adults? Write down evidence from the article to support the view that it is aimed at teenagers.

2 Can you find any evidence to suggest that the article is aimed at adults?

3 Have you reached a final decision about who the target audience is?

Activity 3

12 minutes

Now study the leaflet advertising the Cenarth Adventure Centre on page 27 very carefully and think about the following exam question:

Who is the leaflet aimed at? What evidence can you find to support your answer?

(10 marks)

CENARTH ADVENTURE CENTRE

ALL WEATHER FUN FOR EVERYONE

Open all year

Paintball

Castle Mayhem Outdoor combat Archery

OFF-ROAD RC BUGGIE

Awesome NEW remote-control racing buggies! Our purpose-built short-course track puts you in the driver's seat for intense off-road action!!

ARCHERY

All instruction and coaching is included to make you become a modern Robin Hood. Birthday party packages available.

PAINTBALL RANGE

Have a go with a paintball gun even if you are too young to play, or why not do 'a target practice session' before your paintball game!

WOODLAND CHALLENGE COURSE

Whether you're a group of friends or family, a stag/hen party or a company, you'll enjoy this team activity. The course consists of 12 purpose-built activities such as 'Mission Impossible', 'Minefield' and 'Convicts' Wall'. Who knows – you may even make it onto our champion's leaderboard.

'We all thoroughly enjoyed the team building activities and laser combat. The success of the day is still being talked about!' (Mentor Bro Dinefwr)

GET CREATIVE

From 4 yrs old

Why not 'Get Creative' in our cafe while you sip on a cup of coffee!! Great for all the family or to keep you busy whilst the other family members are taking part in our outdoor activities.

KIDS' CRAFTS
JEWELLLERY MAKING
POTTERING PAINTING
CRAFT PARTY PACKAGES from £10.00pp.
Crafts and food in the cafe. Groups of 10 or more.

PAINTBALL WALL

WALES' PREMIER COMBAT GAME CENTRE

Awesome mission... Castle Mayhem... Military Vehicle... Grenades...

www.cenarth-adventure.co.uk

Award-winning centre

'Good, fun, adrenalin rush, pain, awesome, extreme – really well run.' (*Llandovery College*)

'Fantastic Day' (*Tesco, Cardigan*)

Using the very latest paintball equipment, you could experience the thrill of playing in our very popular 'Castle Mayhem' with two storeys, towers and shields.

CASTLE MAYHEM

SAFETY UKPSF Accredited Centre

The centre has been awarded Accredited Venue status by the United Kingdom Paintball Sports Federation following a vigorous inspection process to ensure players' safety. If a site does not display the accredited venue logo, ask yourself why!

OPEN ALL YEAR	Upgrade gun £3
Min. age 11 years	**PAINTBALLS**
Full day per person	£3.75
Free hot lunch	£6.50
9.30am – 3.30pm approx. times	Boots, gloves, chest protectors available to hire
Half day per person	
9.30am – 12.30pm	For groups of 12+ players £4.50
1pm – 4pm	Paint Grenade

Booking

Booking is essential for all activities to avoid disappointment and session times can vary – PHONE BEFORE YOU TRAVEL! You don't need to be in a group for the combat games, just give us a call and you can join in with others who are up for an exciting game too!

Make sure you wear suitable footwear – boots or old trainers. Prices are correct at time of press.

Please arrive on time for your session. Late arrivals who miss the activity safety briefing will be refused participation. Session times include equipment and safety briefing.

Facilities

The base camp has ample parking, toilets, sheltered reception, large undercover seating area and the Refresh café serving a selection of hot and cold food and drinks – ideal to get refreshed.

www.cenarth-adventure.co.uk   **BOOKING HOTLINE 01559 371621**

1 Remember there can be more than one target audience for a text. Look closely at the advertisement, then fill in the table below to help you organise your ideas.

Target audience	Detail from the text
children	kids' crafts/craft party packages

2 Now write your answer to the question on page 26 in the space below. Remember to find evidence (words/phrase/ pictures) to support the points you make.

12 minutes

_____

_____

_____

_____

_____

_____

_____

_____

_____

_____

_____

_____

3 Look at what you have written and complete this piece of self assessment.

	✓ or ✗	What to include/look for next time
Did you study the writing and the pictures to find the target audience?		
Did you find more than one target audience?		
Did you find any word/phrases to support your points?		

Look at these sample answers to the exam question in Activity 3, written by students in exam conditions.

Student 1

The leaflet is trying to attract everyone to go paintballing. They do this by telling us about lots of activities for everyone and they make it sound like everyone will have lots of fun. There are bright colours which makes it stand out.

Student 2

The leaflet is trying to attract a range of people to go to the centre. I think it attracts people who like adventure and doing exciting things because it is described as an adventure centre which has 'outdoor combat'. It would attract people who are fit and healthy because it sounds like there would be a lot of running around outside. The activities like shooting and archery sound fun but you would have to be quite skilful as well. I think it is also aimed at people who are competitive and like a challenge because it says, 'you could experience the thrill of playing'. It attracts all sorts of people because business people can go there to build team spirit when it says 'groups and corporate'. Men and women can play because it has events for stag and hen parties and even young children because you can play if you are over 5 years old.

1 Now, using the grade descriptions on page vii, award a grade to each answer.
2 What grade would you award to your answer in Activity 3, and why?

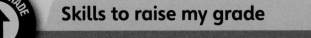

Skills to raise my grade

RAISE MY GRADE

Now you have completed this lesson on intended audience, it's time to fill in the RAG table below to see if your confidence has improved.

	R	A	G
I can recognise a question asking me whom the text is aimed at.	○	○	○
I can understand how to work out the intended audience of a text.	○	○	○
I can organise my answers in a clear and straightforward way.	○	○	○
I can use words and details from the text to support my points.	○	○	○

5 Analysis of persuasive techniques

Skills you need:

You must show that you can:
- recognise persuasive (*how*) questions in the exam
- understand how writers persuade readers
- write about content (*what* is said) and persuasive techniques (*how* it is said)

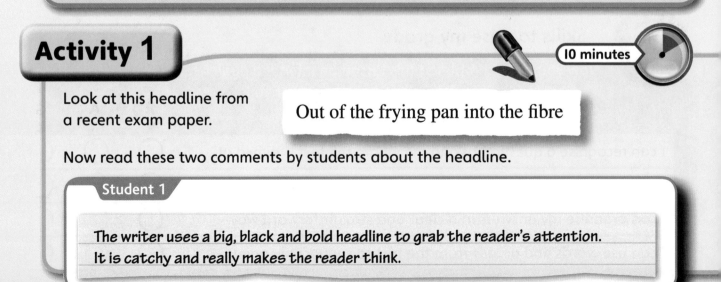

Skills to raise my grade

Fill in the RAG table below to show how confident you are in the following areas:

	R	A	G
I can recognise a persuasive (how) exam question.	○	○	○
I can identify persuasive techniques in texts.	○	○	○
I can organise and write my answers in a clear and straightforward way.	○	○	○
I can include words and phrases from the text to support my points.	○	○	○

Top tips! Persuasion questions

1. Remember to read the question carefully. Underline the key words so you know exactly what you need to look out for.
2. Make sure you are looking at the relevant part of the text – you will not score any marks for information taken from the wrong section.
3. Think about the content of the text (what it is saying) and how the writer is trying to persuade or influence us (the words/techniques being used).
4. Think about the use of headlines, pictures and presentation (how the text is set out on the page).

Activity 1

10 minutes

Look at this headline from a recent exam paper.

> Out of the frying pan into the fibre

Now read these two comments by students about the headline.

Student 1

> The writer uses a big, black and bold headline to grab the reader's attention. It is catchy and really makes the reader think.

Student 2

The writer has deliberately used a well known saying – Out of the frying pan into the fire. This usually means that someone is going from a bad situation into an even worse one. But by saying 'fibre' it makes the reader think that by changing your diet you can go from a bad and unhealthy situation 'the frying pan' into a better and more healthy one 'fibre'.

1 Which answer tells us more about how effective/persuasive the headline is?

Student 1 ☐   Student 2 ☐

Do the same with this next headline.

PLEASE WILL YOU STOP PAYING TO HAVE MY PEOPLE MURDERED?

Student 1

The writer uses dramatic words that appeal to our conscience. It is a shocking headline and immediately makes us feel involved because of the word 'you'. The word 'murdered' is also very shocking and suggests violence and suffering so this makes us wonder what is happening. The headline sounds urgent and desperate because the word 'please' makes it sound like a heartfelt plea.

Student 2

The headline is on top of the page so it stands out. The question is in big writing so we notice it and it means it is asking us a question.

2 Which answer tells us more about how effective/persuasive the headline is?

Student 1 ☐   Student 2 ☐

3 Write down **two** things from this activity that you need to remember when writing about persuasive headlines.

_____

_____

Top tips! Writing about headlines

1 When you write about the effect that headlines have on a reader, you must always be as precise and clear as possible. Find key words in the headline and try to say something about them.

2 You must make your comments specific to the material in front of you. Vague, general comments could refer to any piece of text and will not score you any marks.

3 You may have to write about the presentation or layout of the text, but don't become too sidetracked by this.

4 Always track through the text methodically. Use any bullet points given in the question to organise and structure your answer.

Activity 2

25 minutes

You are going to read the leaflet for International Wildlife Adventures on the opposite page and answer the following exam question.

How does the company try to tempt the reader to go on one of its holidays?
You should comment on:
- **what the company says about itself**
- **what the company says about the holiday**
- **words and phrases used in the text**
- **pictures and layout.**   *(10 marks)*

1 Underline the key words in the question so you know exactly what to focus on, then read the leaflet.

2 Look at the bullet points. How many short paragraphs should you include in your answer?

The Wonders of the Natural World Await You

Our company, International Wildlife Adventures (IWA), was set up for one very special reason: to enable you to experience the amazing natural and wildlife wonders of the world up close in a safe and environmentally responsible way.

We believe that seeing the natural world close up helps us to understand the massive importance of protecting our fragile earth. This is something that can't be adequately achieved by visiting animals in a zoo or watching a wildlife program on television.

Only by experiencing animals in their natural environment can we begin to understand, and appreciate, the delicate balance of our planet.

The Polar Bears of Churchill

Each year, in the fall, along the west shore of Canada's Hudson Bay, one of the world's most fascinating wildlife events occur. Scores of polar bears gather along the shore near Churchill, waiting for the bay to freeze to begin the annual hunt for their choice prey, seals. If you have been fortunate enough to view one of the many television documentaries that feature these Lords of the Arctic, chances are it was filmed in Churchill from one of the original Tundra Buggies. Polar bears are normally solitary creatures, but in Churchill, at this time of year, we can see them gathering, often even mothers and cubs. Wildlife watchers and photographers from all over the world travel to Churchill to witness this remarkable event. As the owners and operators of the original Tundra Buggies, we are able to offer more ways to see polar bears than any other company. In fact, we offer over 60 different options to choose from.

International Wildlife Adventures strongly believe in protecting the bears and their habitat while allowing you the honour of watching them safely from the warmth and comfort of buggies.

Join us to see and photograph the incredible polar bears in Churchill and have an Arctic adventure you will never forget!

The Ultimate Polar Bear Experience:
Tundra Buggy Lodge at Cape Churchill

- *The ultimate polar bear experience*
- *More time with the bear than any other tour*
- *Merv and Lynda Gunter, co-owners of IWA, will be your hosts*
- *Expert professional photographer and naturalist leaders*
- *7 and 8 full days of bear viewing*
- *All meals included*

> Expedition 1:
> November 7–18
>
> From Winnipeg, 8 nights at Tundra Buggy Lodge, 1 night Churchill plus 2 nights hotel in Winnipeg and roundtrip airfare to Churchill.
>
> **Price £3000 per person. All meals included.**

Join us on one of the most unique expeditions on the planet! These trips are based on the shores of Hudson Bay itself, at Cape Churchill. The Cape is the location for the most breathtaking and exciting polar bear photography available. Most of the polar bear documentaries you have seen on TV have been shot on this very trip. Recognised as one of the world's greatest wildlife spectacles, the polar bears of Cape Churchill will take your breath away – and only International Wildlife Adventures can take you there!

Guests will stay in the Tundra Buggy Lodge, our specially designated facility, set up like a train but with a larger-scale interior.

There are open-air platforms, which provide safe viewing and photography areas. The five units consist of two sleeping modules (complete with shared bathroom and show facilities), a lounge module, a dining module, and a module which houses supplies and the camp's power station.

This is a specialist trip and is intended for those interested in the ultimate bear-watching and photography expedition. Experience it yourself with this IWA exclusive. Space is extremely limited on this one-of-a-kind expedition. Reserve your space early.

3 Complete the table below to help you organise your answer to the exam question.

What the company says about itself and the holiday	How does this tempt the reader?
It is environmentally responsible	
	Readers appreciate a solid, reliable company
High quality people involved – professional photographers, etc.	
The holiday is 'unique', and an 'ultimate' holiday. It is a 'specialist' trip	The reader would feel special if they went because not many have this opportunity
Words and phrases used in the text	**How does this tempt the reader?**
	Words like these make the holiday sound like a once-in-a-lifetime experience and opportunity
Description of the bears as 'Lords of the Arctic'	
Pictures and layout	**How does this tempt the reader?**
Images of polar bears	

4 Using all the information you have gathered, write your answer to the exam question in the space below.

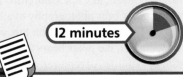

12 minutes

_____

_____

_____

_____

_____

_____

_____

_____

Activity 3

15 minutes

Read the following student answer to the same exam question you answered in Activity 2, written by a student in exam conditions.

Student 1

International Wildlife Adventures tempts the reader with its beaming headlines: 'The Wonders of the World await you'. The company boasts about itself being able to give you a chance to experience natural wildlife wonders close up, in a reasonable manner. They also compare themselves with TV wildlife programmes and zoos.

IWA say their holidays are recognised worldwide and that the polar bears of Cape Churchill will take your breath away. They also explain where people can stay while photographing the bears.

Words and phrases in the text create the right feeling for the reader: 'breathtaking', 'fascinating', 'amazing' – all are words that give the reader a good impression of a unique holiday. They say it's the 'ultimate' holiday or best ever. 'Cape Churchill will take your breath away' is implying that this holiday will be a frightening but exciting experience.

The photographs give the reader a good idea of what kind of sights will be seen. The layout of the headlines written across the page give a sense of organisation to the reader.

This response was awarded 8 marks = Grade C.

1 Using the grade descriptions on page vii, write an examiner comment to explain why it deserves a grade C.

_____

_____

_____

_____

2 Look at what you wrote for your answer in Activity 2. Identify two ways you could improve/add more detail to your response.

_____

_____

Analysis of persuasive techniques

Look at the list of comments below that students have written in response to persuasion-type questions. Some of these comments are very weak because they don't say anything specific about the text and so would not gain any marks.

- The headline is big and black and bold and stands out.
- The headline suggests that the reader will feel directly involved in the experience because of the direct appeal of the word 'you'.
- The writer uses good describing words.
- The use of figures and statistics makes the writer seem knowledgeable and so convinces the reader that the writer has done their research.
- The layout is good.
- The pictures make the leaflet look better.
- There is a lot of information to read.
- The words 'thrilling', 'tremendous', 'stunning' and 'luxury' are all positive and suggest the exceptional nature of the place.
- The use of bold headlines and colourful images help to grab the reader's interest.
- The pictures help to visually describe the experience of the holiday for the reader.

Imagine you were giving advice to your friends about the sort of comments to include in answers to persuasive questions. Decide and tick which of the comments should belong in the 'What to say' column and which should go in the 'What not to say' column.

An example has been done for you.

What to say	What not to say
The headline suggests that the reader will feel directly involved in the experience because of the direct appeal of the word 'you'.	The headline is big and black and bold and stands out.

Look at this student answer which has been written in response to the exam question from Activity 2.

There are several ways in which the company tries to persuade people to go on this trip. The company says it was 'set up for one special reason'. It shows it is a dedicated company. The company 'strongly believes in protecting the bears'. This makes people feel the company cares for what it's doing and values the bears.
The company also says it is 'one of the most unique expeditions on the planet'. This is trying to persuade us that we won't have many chances to do something like this, also saying 'only International Wildlife Adventures can take you there'.

The article is written in the first person which makes it feel like they are talking directly to you. They say 'we offer' and 'join us' which makes the brochure feel personal. They also describe the buggys in detail which gives people a better understanding of the buggys and that they are of a high standard.
The article is split up into sections. The sections are quite small and have different size fonts. This means it doesn't look like too much information and won't put people off. The pictures help as it gives people a better idea of what they will see.

Quote and good comment

Focuses on answering the question

Uses text well to support comments

Attempts to probe the effect of specific words

Answer is well organised

⬜ grade

1 Award the answer a grade in the box above.
2 Annotate the answer by matching up the comment boxes with points in the answer.

RAISE MY GRADE

Skills to raise my grade

Now you have completed this lesson on analysing persuasive techniques, it's time to fill in the RAG table below to see if your confidence has improved.

	R	A	G
I can recognise a persuasive (*how*) exam question.	○	○	○
I can identify persuasive techniques in texts.	○	○	○
I can organise and write my answers in a clear and straightforward way.	○	○	○
I can include words from the text to support my points.	○	○	○

Skills you need:

You must show that you can:
- recognise and understand compare and contrast questions
- compare and contrast two texts
- organise material in a logical way to help write answers clearly

Skills to raise my grade

Fill in the RAG table below to show how confident you are in the following areas:

	R	A	G
I can recognise a comparison question.	○	○	○
I can select the material I need from both reading texts.	○	○	○
I can organise and write my answers in a clear and straightforward way.	○	○	○
I can focus on the material in front of me and not give my own opinion in the answer.	○	○	○

Top tips! Compare and contrast questions

1 Always read the question carefully. You are being asked to find similarities and differences between the two texts. You are **not** being asked to give your opinion, so do not waste time by doing this.
2 Follow the instructions in the question. You will usually be given bullet points to follow, and you should try to write a paragraph about each one. Sometimes you will be told to write your answer under certain headings. This will help you to organise your material carefully.
3 The examiners are trying to help you get a good grade, so do exactly what they are asking you to do!

Activity 1

3 minutes

In order to check that you understand exactly what a question is asking you to do, can you explain what the following words/phrases mean?

	Explanation
Compare	
Contrast	
Make cross reference	

Top tips! Answering compare questions

1 Underline the key words in the question and bullet points so you know exactly what information to look for.

2 Make sure you are looking at the correct part of the texts – you will not score any marks for information taken from the wrong section.

3 Work your way through the text, line by line, so you don't miss any points or information that will help you answer the question. Underline or highlight each point as you find it.

4 Make sure you have answered **all** the bullet points in the question if you hope to score full marks.

5 Only spend 12 or 13 minutes writing your answer for questions like this.

Activity 2

20 minutes

You are going to read two texts about a holiday camp: 'Marchants Hill' and 'Home or Away?' on pages 40–41. First, read the following exam question.

> **Compare the ways the two texts tell you about a PGL holiday.**
> **You must include comments on:**
> • **who each text is aimed at**
> • **in what ways each text would help you to choose a holiday.** *(10 marks)*

1 Highlight the key words in the exam question.

2 Now read the two texts on pages 40–41 and underline/highlight points that you could use in your answer.

3 How many paragraphs could you include in your answer to make sure you have covered **all** the bullet points?

4 This particular question has not given you any headings to help you organise your answer. Can you think of a suitable heading for each short paragraph?

Marchants Hill

The greatest way to spend the school holidays...ever!

If you're looking for excitement, wanting to make new friends or enjoy the freedom to express yourself, then you're looking in the right place! At PGL you'll have the opportunity to try as many activities as possible, have loads of fun and learn new skills and tricks along the way – guaranteed!

There's never a dull moment – day or night! Choose to go all out on a multi-activity holiday or choose one of our unique specialist holidays. Come for a day, a mini break or full week (or even two!). Try our new introductory breaks or celebrate your birthday with us. Come alone or come with friends...whatever you choose to do, you'll be zorbing, surfing or abseiling and having a barrel of laughs in no time!

So for your perfect holiday read on...

WHAT'S IT LIKE?

At Marchants Hill there are 45 acres of grounds packed with activities so everything is just a short walk away. As well as recently constructed accommodation, dining room and sports hall, there are over 20 activities all situated on site! It's great for all ages and there's a big range of holidays to choose from.

WHAT'S THE ACCOMMODATION LIKE?

Our fantastic accommodation blocks sleep 6 in each room and all are en-suite. 13–16's are mainly accommodated in our adjoining annexe, Bethany House, which has en-suite and 6–8 bedded rooms. It's a couple of minutes' walk away with its own dining room, tuck shop and separate chill-out room away from our younger guests.

WHAT FACILITIES ARE THERE?

Opened by Dame Kelly Holmes, our fantastic sports and activity hall offers even more great activities – inside and out.

For 13–16-year-olds there's a chill-out room with TV, CD player and pool table – a great place to relax with your friends.

In the grounds there are 3 abseil towers, 3 zip wires, 2 low ropes courses, 2 challenge courses, 3 trapezes as well as a giant swing, motorsports track, archery range and a huge multi-activity tower.

With more than 50 years' experience pioneering children's adventure and activity holidays, our mission has always been to provide children with a unique mix of 'adventure, freedom and friendship', delivered in a safe and caring environment.

PGL kids everywhere will tell you that we are the best when it comes to thrills, challenges and adventures wrapped up with tons of fun into one mega holiday.

THE TIMES

HOME OR AWAY?

What to do with the kids in the holidays

Andrew Purvis writes about the week his two children, Lawrence and Rosie, spent on a PGL holiday.

In the last week of the school holiday we drove to Marchants Hill in Surrey, the nearest PGL centre to our home in London. The crude wooden dormitories, toilet and washing blocks, flagpole and assault course made it look like an army barracks. The camp, with its wooden huts (referred to in the brochure as 'chalets') had been used for children evacuated from London during the Second World War.

After a quick tour with a group leader, slightly spoiled by a girl older than my two weeping loudly as her parents left, the Big Moment for Leaving came. Lawrence, nine, had already found a friend and was on to the next thing (orange juice and games). 'Bye, Dad,' he said, then disappeared. Rosie, nearly two years younger, looked at me mistrustfully. There was a slight wobble of the lip but the next moment she was off, sprinting excitedly towards the meeting point where the rising babble of a hundred children's voices made me glad I was getting in the car and going home. But it was a difficult moment. Entrusting your children to complete strangers for a week is not easy. As I turned out of the camp, they were out of sight but not out of mind.

What they did in the next seven days is a complete mystery, the only details coming from the journals they kept and odd conversations, punctuated by squeals of laughter, about events half-remembered. Lawrence was enrolled on the specialist 'Newsflash' course – film-making, photography and magazine production. Half of each day was spent taking part in climbing, archery and mountain biking. In his journal he wrote, 'Monday: Newsflash was good. We made a video. It was great. Anybody who likes climbing or computers should choose Newsflash.' Rosie chose the multi-activity programme – lots of sports and rowdy games at the centre's two activity zones – the Lookout and Coppice Corner. While Lawrence shared a small room with three other boys, Rosie slept in a large dormitory.

Three subjects kept cropping up in their journals. The first was the amount of technology from the dozens of computers, cameras and microphones on the Newsflash course, to the state-of-the-art archery equipment. The second was the zany singsongs every night, songs which Rosie sang for weeks afterwards. The other subject was discipline, which by their account was very strict. They were woken up every day 'very early', told to dress and then assembled on a patch of grass with a strange wooden totem pole at its centre.

When I collected the children the next Saturday, they were boisterous, sunkissed and filthy. Their rucksacks were full of sodden towels, other people's clothing and a riverbed of mud. They had loved it. I couldn't understand why they were shouting. Then it dawned on me: if you live for a week with a hundred children, you forget what a normal voice sounds like. Never mind assault courses and abseiling towers, Sunday breakfast was going to be the real challenge.

5 Now spend 12 minutes writing your answer in the space provided below.

Activity 3

15 minutes

Now read the three student answers below, which were written in response to the exam question given in Activity 2, under exam conditions.

Student 1

Both of the texts are aimed at the parents and the purpose of the brochure is to persuade you to send your children on the holiday where as the purpose of the article is to inform you of the parents point of view although in the article he does promote it by saying that his children enjoyed their time at the camp. In both the article and the brochure the children involved look or sound as though they are having fun.

Student 2

The brochure and Andrew Purvis' account are very different, the brochure is trying to promote the place and the Andrew Purvis account is trying to tell an accurate tale of what it is like.

The brochure is tried to be aimed at the children, to try and make them want to go. I think this because the brochure is bright colours with plenty of pictures of the activities available and children looking like they are having a good time.

The Andrew Purvis account is tried to be aimed at the parents with no pictures and a rather dull colour in the background.

The brochure doesn't have any words by children saying that they enjoyed themselves, however the picture have been cleverly chosen and given the impression that they are having a good time and enjoying themselves.

This has a good comparison with the Andrew Purvis account. Where his two children has a great time and enjoyed themselves.

Student 3

The Article that Andrew wrote was definitely aimed for an adult audience just to show them his point of view on the camp and the holiday his children went on.

The brochure is aimed at the varied audience and is purposly made for adults and children. They have added lots of colour which would attract a child's attention. Also they have added picture as a visual effect. This brochure is trying to attract costumers and to inform they about the place. The fact that the children has so much fun and enjoyed themselves would mean a lot to a reader who was wondering whether to send his child on PGL holiday. The article is also based on a non-bias view which is really important to a reader.

The fact that all the children are smiling on the picture in the brochure is reassuring because it points out that the children really do enjoy themselves and have a lot of fun. The way in which the children react in both the article and the brochure would help make my decision on a holiday because they are the ones who actually went there and experienced it.

However to finalise my opinion I would have to look at the brochure and take note of all the facts they have included so I knew exactly what was going on there i.e. the safety aspects and the activity systems.

1 Mark on the line where you think each student answer belongs.

Strongest   Weakest

2 What is needed to improve Student I's response? Suggest **two** things.

3 How would you improve Student 2's answer to make it more detailed?

4 Write down **two** things that make Student 3's answer effective.

Activity 4

5 minutes

To check that you understand about comparing and contrasting questions, write down a list of **five** things you need to do in order to answer questions like these.

15 minutes

MAKE THE GRADE · MAKE THE GRADE

You are going to read the articles 'Banana Campaign Sheet' and 'We're all going bananas' below and on page 46. First, look at the following exam question.

Compare and contrast the newspaper article and the campaign sheet, using these headings:
- **the purpose of each article**
- **how the content is similar**
- **how the content is different.**

(10 marks)

Banana Campaign sheet
The latest information and ideas for action

Bananas are the UK's most popular fruit and the most valuable food product sold in British supermarkets. Yet banana farmers and workers around the world face extremely difficult and often dangerous working conditions. Bananas carrying the FAIRTRADE Mark are now available in Britain. This mark guarantees that the producers have had a better deal.

Cheap and cheerful?

Bananas may be cheap and popular with the consumer, but they are cheap partly because of the conditions under which they are grown. Large companies control the plantations in Latin America where the cheapest bananas are produced, but the social and environmental costs of achieving high levels of productivity are huge. The over-use of agricultural chemical damages the environment and the health of the people exposed to them. Some 20% of the male banana workers in Costa Rica have been left sterile after handling toxic chemicals, while women in packing plants suffer double the national rate of leukaemia.

As well as being forced to endure appalling working conditions, plantation workers are also paid very poor wages. Some farmers are getting very low prices for their bananas. These can be as low as $2 for a 40lb box (3p per pound) – which does not even cover the cost of production. The result is that many poor farmers are losing money, and as a result are gradually losing their livelihoods.

Fairtrade bananas are packaged with the FAIRTRADE Mark and this guarantees that producers are paid a fair price for their goods. Many shoppers are willing to buy Fairtrade bananas even though they cost a bit more. Over a third of the EU population said they would be prepared to pay a little more for a Fairtrade product. More than 70% of UK shoppers say they care about the conditions endured by the people who produce goods for them to consume.

Look for the FAIRTRADE Mark if you want to be sure the producers get a fair deal.

Supermarket action

In order for producers to benefit from Fairtrade it is crucial that Fairtrade bananas sell well. They are available in most Sainsbury's and Co-op supermarkets and early indications are that sales have been very good. However, some of the other supermarkets are currently considering whether to stock them too. The more widely available Fairtrade bananas are, the more people are likely to buy them, and the more producers will benefit – please let your supermarket know that their customers want to buy Fairtrade!

What can you do to support Fairtrade?

If a supermarket in your area stocks Fairtrade bananas:
- Publicise Fairtrade bananas – tell friends about them.
- Buy Fairtrade bananas regularly, otherwise they will rot on supermarket shelves and will soon be dropped by the supermarket.
- Tell people to look for the FAIRTRADE Mark, and let them know what it stands for.

If your local supermarket store hasn't already got Fairtrade bananas:
- Please ask for them! Customer comments cards and suggestions books are read carefully by managers, and do influence decisions. Alternatively, ask the Customer Services Desk when they will have them, and leave your address so that they can get their head office's response to you.

Get others to do the same. Supermarkets like to meet their customers' demands.

Thank you!

Live the difference – buy Fairtrade products

We're all going bananas

Sales of bananas have reached an all-time high, eclipsing the simple British apple in our affections. Robin McKie reports on the soaring popularity of this country's favourite, life-enhancing fruit.

BRITAIN HAS GONE bananas. Over the past 12 months we have consumed an unprecedented 3.5 billion pieces of fruit, forcing our native apple into a poor second place.

The banana is healthy, the ideal snack food if fitness is a priority. It is packed with energy, fibre and vitamins. It is rich in potassium and low in calories. And eating two bananas provides enough energy for a strenuous 90-minute workout. Sportsmen like Tiger Woods and the entire Manchester United team, who eat banana and jam sandwiches before games, rely on the fruit to maintain their sporting prowess.

The nation's banana boom is one of the most remarkable of recent years, a guide not just to the impact of healthy-eating campaigns but also to the country's economic health. We spend more money on bananas than any other supermarket item apart from petrol and lottery tickets, and more than 95 per cent of our households buy them every week. Bananas are us, it seems.

The addiction will be reinforced this month as viewers watch endless Wimbledon shots of tennis players munching their way through hundreds of bananas, a fruit now considered necessary for recovery between sets and rallies.

Yet a century ago hardly anyone in Britain had tasted or even seen a banana. Early attempts to bring them to Britain met with failure because by the time they had been picked, packaged and then shipped, they had rotted beyond recognition. The development of refrigerated shipping changed everything, with the first shipment arriving 100 years ago this month, triggering a national love affair from which we have never looked back.

A striking measure of the banana's popularity can be seen in trade figures that show sales in the UK have rocketed by more than 150 per cent since 1985, while fruit sales in general have risen by a mere 15 per cent. Last year alone there was a 9 per cent growth in British banana sales.

'The banana has everything going for it, so its popularity should not seem that surprising,' said Lyndsey Morgan of the fruit's marketing organisation, the Banana Group.

'It is easy to open and is a high-energy food. It is also a first class hangover cure, stabilises blood pressure and soothes heartburn. And when you want to start weaning babies, mashed banana is the perfect food. You can even use the skins as garden fertiliser when you have finished. It is astonishingly versatile.'

Bananas are seen as a symbol of economic strength because countries that buy them in the largest quantities are always wealthy nations, like Britain. However, there is a downside to the banana's popularity. As campaign groups like Fairtrade point out, banana plantation workers are usually very poorly paid. Many live in miserable housing in near-starvation and are left sterile by the use of chemicals in banana production.

As a result, some supermarkets such as Sainsbury's now offer Fairtrade bananas, which have been bought directly from the growers, who are guaranteed a realistic price for their products. Such schemes are already helping farmers in Costa Rica, Ghana, and St Vincent. Some 10,000 tonnes of Fairtrade bananas were sold in Britain last year, but this represents only a fraction of our supermarket sales. Last year 725,000 tonnes were sold in Britain.

Crucially, increasing numbers of these bananas are being specially packaged – for example, in kids' packs, using smaller fruit, or in 'Eat me/Keep me' bags in which fruit at different stages of ripeness is sold to help once-a-week shoppers.

It is this kind of aggressive marketing that has helped keep the banana at the forefront of British shopping and command a place in virtually every household.

Annual consumption now stands at the equivalent of two bananas a week for every man, woman and child in the British Isles, an annual trade now valued at more than £600 million.

1 Using the information you have read, write your answer in paragraph using the headings you have been given in the exam question on page 45.

_____

_____

_____

_____

_____

_____

_____

_____

_____

_____

_____

_____

_____

_____

_____

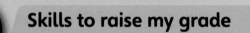

Skills to raise my grade

Now you have completed this lesson on comparison of texts, it's time to fill in the RAG table below to see if your confidence has improved.

	R	A	G
I can recognise a comparison question.	○	○	○
I can select the material I need from both reading texts.	○	○	○
I can organise and write my answers in a clear and straightforward way.	○	○	○
I can focus on the material in front of me and not give my own opinion in the answer.	○	○	○

2 Writing information and ideas

Writing mark scheme

Content and organisation (13 marks)

C grade answer

(8–13 marks)

- You know exactly what you are being asked to do in your writing.
- You know exactly who you are writing for and have thought about what will interest that person or group.
- Your work is long enough and you have covered a number of points in detail.
- Your writing has paragraphs and the structure makes sense.

- You have used a good variety of carefully chosen words.
- You have thought carefully about why you are writing, and who you are writing for, and have adapted your style to suit them.
- You have got all the details of the appropriate audience correct.

E grade answer

(5–8 marks)

- You have some idea of what you are supposed to be writing about.
- Your layout is partially correct, but could be improved.
- You have begun to give some evidence or support for what you are writing.

- You have given some structure to your writing so that it makes some sense.
- You have begun to think about what will interest your audience.
- Your vocabulary is not limited to simple words.

G grade answer

(1–5 marks)

- Some of your work shows you know who you are writing for and there is a little formatting.
- You show only a very limited understanding of how to write for a particular audience.
- Your work is too short and not all of it is relevant to the task.

- Your ideas are mostly in a sensible order.
- You use a couple of paragraphs but you do not show much understanding of how a paragraph should be used.
- The way you have written does not show much evidence that you know for who you are writing for.
- Your range of vocabulary is rather limited. You are only using simple words.

Sentence structure, punctuation and spelling *(7 marks)*

C grade answer

(5–7 marks)

- You use a lot of different kinds of sentences and sentence openings.
- You have made very few, if any, mistakes with your full stops, commas and apostrophes.

- You make very few, if any, spelling mistakes.
- You keep to one tense and you do not make mistakes with subject/verb agreement. You use a singular verb with a singular subject and a plural verb with a plural subject.

E grade answer

(3–4 marks)

- You have used a number of different sentence openings and structures.
- Most of your punctuation is correct, though you may have made one or two mistakes with full stops, commas and apostrophes.

- Most of your spelling, even of more difficult words, is correct.
- Generally you keep to one tense and you do not make mistakes with subject/verb agreement. You use a singular verb with a singular subject and a plural verb with a plural subject.

G grade answer

(1–2 marks)

- You have only used very simple sentence structures.
- You have made a number of mistakes in the way you have used commas, full stops and apostrophes.

- Most of your spelling is correct but you make mistakes with simple words.
- You have not been consistent in your tenses and sometimes you have, for example, used a singular verb with a plural subject (for example, 'We was going').

7 Informal letters

Skills to raise my grade

Fill in the RAG table below to show how confident you are in the following areas:

	R	A	G
I can organise my ideas in an appropriate form.	○	○	○
I can write sentences and paragraphs in a logical sequence.	○	○	○
I can use a variety of sentence structures and a range of vocabulary.	○	○	○
I can use punctuation accurately.	○	○	○
I know how to recognise a task which requires an informal letter.	○	○	○

Top tips! Informal letter writing

1 Your audience will usually be family, close friends and people you know well.
2 Your purpose is to provide them with information, entertain them or give them friendly advice.
3 Your language can be informal and relaxed, but don't use text language or slang.
4 Your tone should be friendly.
5 In the exam you will be expected to set out your letter correctly and you will either be given an address or told to use your own.

Activity 1

3 minutes

Decide whether these situations use formal or informal language.

	FORMAL	INFORMAL
1 Job application letter		
2 Letter to a sick friend in hospital		
3 Letter complaining about a faulty washing machine		
4 Letter to a newspaper in response to an article		
5 Letter to a relative, thanking him/her for a birthday gift		
6 Letter to a travel agent, complaining about the poor standard of holiday accommodation		

1 Using the suggestions below, label the features of an informal letter.

- Middle part of the letter and all of the details
- Opening paragraph
- Concluding paragraph to emphasise your points
- Address of person who is writing the letter
- Greeting
- Signature
- Date
- Informal ending

Informal letters

You will usually write an informal letter to a family member or a friend, so think carefully about how you would begin and end your letter.

Activity 3

4 minutes

Decide which of these greetings and endings would be most appropriate in a letter written to the following people. Number your choices 1–3, with 1 being your top choice.

Letter to a grandparent:

Greetings grandparent		With love	
Dear Nan		Yours faithfully	
Dearest grandmother		Catch you soon	

Letter to a best friend:

To my best friend		See you soon	
Whassup		Best wishes	
Hi		Yours truly	

Letter to a brother/sister:

Dear …		CUL8er	
Hey sis/bro		Yours sincerely	
Hello sister/brother		Love	

Activity 4

25 minutes

Read the exam question below:

> **Your friend is in hospital recovering from a broken leg. Write a cheerful, lively and entertaining letter to your friend to cheer them up.** *(20 marks)*

1 Read the grade C description on page 48 and jot down what you need to include in your answer.

2 Now answer the exam question, using the scaffolding opposite to help you.

First paragraph

Ask your friend some questions about how they are feeling and what life is like in hospital. You could write about how you found out about their accident.

Second paragraph

Describe what you have been doing, some of the things that have happened at home or some of the gossip from events at school which will be interesting to them.

Third paragraph

Suggest something you and your friend can do once they have recovered. Give all the details about where you will go and what you will do.

Final paragraph

Explain when you will visit and wish them a speedy recovery.

Informal letters

Activity 5

10 minutes

Complete this checklist for informal letters to help with your revision.

Layout feature

- Address of writer in top right-hand corner _____
- _____
- _____
- _____
- _____

Language feature

- Informal tone _____
- _____
- _____
- _____
- _____

Accurate writing

- Spelling is mostly correct _____
- _____
- _____
- _____
- _____

Remember that in the exam:

- You have 30 minutes to complete the question.
- The question is worth 20 marks. 7 of these marks are for sentence structure, punctuation and spelling, so check your writing very carefully.
- You will be expected to write approximately 1–2 sides in your answer booklet.
- Don't use text language or slang because you will lose marks.

Read the grade D letter below, which was written in response to this exam question:

> **Your friend has decided to run the London marathon. Write a cheerful, lively and entertaining letter to your friend to advise and encourage them while they are training.** *(20 marks)*

D grade answer

Dear Jack,

I was told Recently that you are planning on running in the London marathon and I would like to say go for it mate. You were always the fittest in school and you enjoy long distances so this is the event for you. From what I've herd this run is about twenty six miles long to be honest I don't think I could run six, let alone twenty six and since you only have one month to prepare here is a list of things you can do to get ready for the big race.

- eat healthily because if you eat unhealthily your fitness will deteriorate and make the marathon harder than it already is.
- Jog every day gradually increasing the speeds and lengths so that you are ready for the length of the marathon
- And the day before eat plenty of cakes so you have stored energy

Though I do advise you don't overdo it. If you feel pain or sickness during the race then pull out, I don't want a good friend being injured because of a silly run.

Write back soon

Sam

Content and organisation

1 Write down **two** positive points about the letter.

2 Write down **two** negative points about the letter.

Sentence structure, punctuation and spelling

3 Write down **two** positive points about the letter.

4 Write down **two** negative points about the letter.

5 Write down five ways that you would improve this letter from a grade D to a grade C using the grade descriptions on pages 48–9.

6 Now write your own informal letter in response to the exam question below.

> Write a letter to your older brother/sister who has recently moved away to study at university. Write them a letter in which you tell them some news about the family or school and also try to persuade them to come home for the holidays. *(20 marks)*

_____

_____

_____

_____

_____

_____

_____

_____

_____

_____

_____

_____

_____

_____

_____

_____

_____

_____

RAISE MY GRADE

Skills to raise my grade

Now you have completed this lesson on informal letters, it's time to fill in the RAG table below to see if your confidence has improved.

	R	A	G
I can organise my ideas in an appropriate form.	◯	◯	◯
I can write sentences and paragraphs in a logical sequence.	◯	◯	◯
I can use a variety of sentence structures and a range of vocabulary.	◯	◯	◯
I can use punctuation accurately.	◯	◯	◯
I can recognise tasks which require an informal letter response.	◯	◯	◯

Skills you need:

You must show that you can:
- set out formal letters correctly
- adopt the right tone and formal style
- understand the differences between formal and informal letters

RAISE MY GRADE

Skills to raise my grade

Fill in the RAG table below to show how confident you are in the following areas:

	R	A	G
I can write in a formal style.	○	○	○
I can write sentences and paragraphs in a logical sequence.	○	○	○
I can use a variety of sentence structures and a range of vocabulary.	○	○	○
I can spell most words correctly and punctuate accurately.	○	○	○
I can recognise tasks which require a formal letter response.	○	○	○

Top tips! Formal letter writing

1   Your audience will usually be someone you do not know or someone you don't know very well. This could be a potential employer, a newspaper editor, a headteacher or a member of the local council.
2   Your purpose could be to make a complaint about something, to apply for a job or to give your point of view in a persuasive way.
3   Your language needs to be formal and polite, with no slang or text language.
4   Your tone needs to be firm but polite and serious. You cannot be chatty or rude here!
5   In the exam you will be expected to set out your letter correctly.

Activity 1

10 minutes

1   Read the letter opposite carefully. It is written by a headteacher to parents. Highlight or underline all the words/phrases that are inappropriate.

St Kevin's School

Silver Avenue, Surehampton, England ES45 7GD

22nd March 2011

Hello Hugo's Mum and Dad,

I'm afraid your little Hugo has been up to his old tricks again! His messing about has landed him in a whole heap of trouble.

Mrs Stern is well mad. You should have seen her when she saw Hugo's handiwork painted on the wall of the canteen. She aint no Beyonce, but that painting made her look proper rough. Its like he is chucking the school rules in our face.

As if that was not enough, the icing on the cake came in science. Tommy is still recovering at St Maggies, the docs are still not sure how to get the test tube off his finger safely. Hugo has been a real pain.

After a chat with the governors, I'm afraid you're not going to be happy. We don't want him back until next term. This gives him time to think about all this stuff. I would also like it if you popped in for a chin wag about Hugo's future at St Kev's.

Speak to you later.

From

Ian Dally

---

2 Write down alternative words and phrases that would be more appropriate to use in a formal letter.

_____

_____

_____

_____

Activity 2

15 minutes

1 Using the suggestions below, label the features of the formal letter on truancy.

- Date
- Greeting
- Final paragraph to state the action expected as a result of the letter
- Address of person writing the letter
- Middle part of letter giving the main arguments and details

- Opening paragraph giving reasons for writing
- Signature
- Name of writer printed
- Address of person reading the letter
- Signing off

137 Queen Street
Longfield
Swindon
SN44 2NT

17th February 2011

The Editor
The Times
London
SW12 5BH

Dear Sir/Madam

After recently reading an article about the frightening increase in truancy rates in Britain, I feel compelled to offer my views on the subject. I was shocked and surprised at the astoundingly high number of students who truant every day.

As a Year 11 student at Blanksville Comprehensive School, I feel frightened at the waste that I see around me. Thousands and thousands of teenagers are throwing away their education and are destroying their futures. I feel that something has to be done quickly to stop the growing problem from spiralling out of control.

I truly believe that boring lessons are a major factor of truancy. Too much theory and copying out of textbooks instead of taking part in practical lessons makes it all very tedious. If students become too bored they will play truant, fall behind with vital work and miss out on future opportunities.

Also, I firmly believe that bullying is a massive factor in truancy. Students who are bullied, both mentally and physically, may be forced to escape from the bullies in the only way they know how – by not attending school.

Many students across the country think they are simply 'too cool' to attend school and, of course, linked to this problem is peer pressure. There is also evidence that clearly shows that levels of truancy are higher in the summer months when children would rather be outside in the sunshine with their friends than sitting in a cramped, stuffy classroom. Other students just skip off lessons for the thrill, or to get attention or simply just to rebel against authority.

Without a doubt, a lack of decent resources like computers and textbooks may lead people into truanting because there is so little incentive to complete assignments.

Surely, we all want the best education for the children of this country? I am sure you will agree that truancy will have a major effect on our country's future unless something is done to combat the situation now! Obviously you are aware that there is a proven link between truancy, juvenile crime and anti social behaviour.

With a staggering 200,000 students truanting every day, I am confident you'll agree that we must do everything we can to solve this growing problem.

Yours faithfully,

H.D. Smith

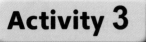

Activity 3

 25 minutes

1 Using the planning template below, write a letter to your local council complaining about the lack of facilities for young people in your local area.

You should aim to write a grade C letter, so read the description on page 48 to make sure you know how to achieve a grade C.

Formal layout
Set out your letter correctly using formal letter layout. Make up any details needed, such as names and addresses.

First paragraph
Make it clear why you are writing. What exactly are you complaining about?

Second paragraph
Develop your points in the best possible order. Put your strongest/most serious point first for impact.

Final paragraph
What action do you expect the council to take as a result of your letter? End and sign off your letter in the appropriate way.

Activity 4

Read the following letter in which a student writes to their headteacher about the decision to allow girls to play in the boys' football team.

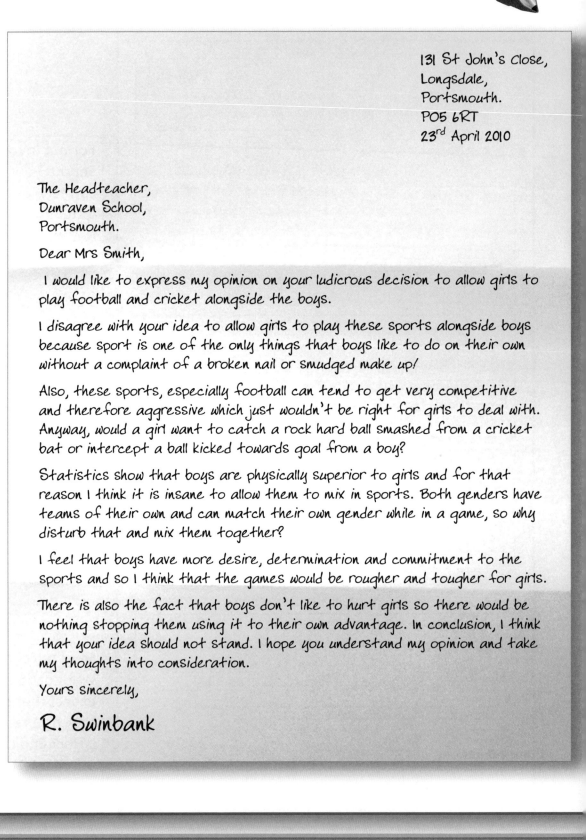

131 St John's Close,
Longsdale,
Portsmouth.
PO5 6RT
23rd April 2010

The Headteacher,
Dunraven School,
Portsmouth.

Dear Mrs Smith,

I would like to express my opinion on your ludicrous decision to allow girls to play football and cricket alongside the boys.

I disagree with your idea to allow girls to play these sports alongside boys because sport is one of the only things that boys like to do on their own without a complaint of a broken nail or smudged make up!

Also, these sports, especially football can tend to get very competitive and therefore aggressive which just wouldn't be right for girls to deal with. Anyway, would a girl want to catch a rock hard ball smashed from a cricket bat or intercept a ball kicked towards goal from a boy?

Statistics show that boys are physically superior to girls and for that reason I think it is insane to allow them to mix in sports. Both genders have teams of their own and can match their own gender while in a game, so why disturb that and mix them together?

I feel that boys have more desire, determination and commitment to the sports and so I think that the games would be rougher and tougher for girls.

There is also the fact that boys don't like to hurt girls so there would be nothing stopping them using it to their own advantage. In conclusion, I think that your idea should not stand. I hope you understand my opinion and take my thoughts into consideration.

Yours sincerely,

R. Swinbank

1 Write down an example of a polite tone in the letter.

2 Write down an example of a strong opinion in the letter.

3 Find an example of a rhetorical question.

4 Find an example of persuasive statistics.

5 Find an exclamation mark for dramatic effect.

6 Write down **two** things that the student does well in the letter.

7 Write down **two** things that the student needs to improve in the letter.

Here are two formal letters written by students in response to the exam question below:

> A local restaurant is advertising for part-time staff. Write a letter to the manager
> of the restaurant in response to the advertisement. *(20 marks)*

1 Annotate the two letters to explain the differences between the D grade and C grade letters.

Dear Sir/madame.
    I am applying for your advertisement on part-time staff. I
have had experience in this type of work and enjoy it. Im a very well
organised polite and good with people. I find that I am quick on my
feet and react well in emergancies. I am calm and have a good sense
of humour. I enjoy working as a team and cope well under preasure.

I live near by so getting to the hotel/restaurant would not be a
problem. I grew up in a hotel as my parents owned one for 15
years so I got a chance to learn the in's and out's of hotle life from
cleaning to managment.

I have done work experience also in a hotle as a waitress and
barstaff and found it rather intresting.

I belive that my future career will involve hotle/restaurnts and I
think this will be a great place for me to start.

I am about to start a part time course at college in hospitality and
hotel management so I belive that this job would be a great kick
start to my aims in life and to my future carreer. The more work
experience I get out of work in a hotel, the more chance I will get of
getting furthur in life. I realy think im the person for you, we would
both benefit from this

Thank you very much

Yours sincerly
Zac Oblyschuk

Dear Mr Bradley,

I would like to take this opportunity to present you with my letter of application.

I have seen the advertisement for the part-time staff you are requiring which was placed in the 'Grands' front window.

I am 18 years old currently training to become a nurse at Smithfield college. I successfully passed my GCSEs at school with grade Cs and above, which has greatly helped me to complete my course at college.

I feel I am hard working and ambitious and I will complete a given task to the best of my ability. I feel I would suit this job as I am good at communicating with the public and since I am cheerful I love to get on with people.

I've worked in a local shop in my village so I can handle money and can use a till. My father also has a business and I work for him when he's busy, mainly answering the phone, producing invoices and general office essentials.

In my spare time I like to play sport, mainly hockey and generally keep fit. I have a car and I love to see new places and visit friends and family. That is an advantage as I won't need to rely on public transport to get me to work on time.

I do hope you concider me as a new employee. Please contact me anytime on 0206 123 3636.

Yours sincerely
Leila Abu-Rish

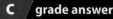

Skills to raise my grade

Now you have completed this lesson on formal letters, it's time to fill in the RAG table below to see if your confidence has improved.

	R	A	G
I can write in a formal style.	○	○	○
I can write sentences and paragraphs in a logical sequence.	○	○	○
I can use a variety of sentence structures and a range of vocabulary.	○	○	○
I can spell most words correctly and punctuate accurately.	○	○	○
I can recognise tasks which require a formal letter response.	○	○	○

9 Reports

Skills to raise my grade

RAISE MY GRADE

Fill in the RAG table below to show how confident you are in the following areas:

	R	A	G
I can sequence my ideas so my report sounds logical and organised.	○	○	○
I can write about my ideas and information coherently.	○	○	○
I can divide my points into clear topic areas based on the subject of the report.	○	○	○
I can spell and use punctuation correctly.	○	○	○

Activity 1

6 minutes

Read the following list of statements about report writing and decide which are true and which are false. Write your answers in the empty column below.

Statement	True or False?
1 The purpose of a report is to entertain the reader	
2 The purpose of a report is to provide the reader with information	
3 A report has lots of pictures to grab the attention of the reader	
4 A report should be clearly organised into logical paragraphs	
5 It is helpful to use subheadings to introduce your ideas in a report	
6 A report should be written in columns like a newspaper	
7 You should use a lively and chatty tone when writing a report	
8 Reports are usually written in the present tense	
9 If you use facts/statistics in your report, make sure they are realistic and believable	
10 Reports should be written in standard English	

Top tips! Report writing

1 Always read the question carefully. It helps if you underline or highlight the key words to decide on the purpose (**why** you are writing the report) and the audience (**who** will read it).
2 Remember that the purpose of a report is generally to give information.
3 Reports are written for a particular audience and should explain clearly what you think they need to know about a specific topic.
4 When thinking about your content you should select only what is relevant and important.
5 Try to organise your facts/ideas under different headings so the reader can understand easily.
6 Write your ideas in a clear and straightforward style.
7 Your audience will vary, but the exam question will always make clear which person, group of people or organisation your report is aimed at. This must influence what you include in your report.

Activity 2

5 minutes

Read Student I's report on page 68. It is written to a headteacher about ways in which facilities in school could be improved for Year II students.

This report is not perfect but there are some good points.

1 Write down **three** things that the report does well.

- _____
- _____
- _____

2 What would you do to improve the report? Write down **three** areas for improvement.

- _____
- _____
- _____

<u>Improving the image</u>
Leaking ceilings, drab colours, depressing moods, dirty floors, plain surroundings
... these are just a few of the compliants of the past and present year 11
students who are looking for the enthusiasm and motivation needed for their
gcse exams. At this present time, year 11 are faced with weeks of monotinous
revision and borring lessons and to make matters worse they have to do this in
dull, plain and glum classrooms. It is important to get rid of this bordom because
happy students get the best results. To stop this problem I suggest that
classrooms should be brightned up with colours and posters on the walls

<u>Revision time</u>
Another masive problem facing year 11 students is finding time to revise
without interuptions. Many students have said it is dificult to revise at home
because of the noise of family, tv and music. Students should have time to do
there own revision in school. I would find this usful.
Another problem is when and were students can have this revision time. There is
nowere to go at lunch or after school. So it would be a goodidea to make a library
and classroom availible to students.

<u>Extra lessons</u>
One other problem faced by year 11 students is not understanding the work
and not having the oppitunity for extra help. Therefore it would be a good idea to
offer revision classes to those who want it.

I hope you will think about my ideas about dull and boring classrooms, little
revision time and revision classes.

Yours sincerely,
Jane Briggs

Activity 3

5 minutes

Read this second report from another student on the same topic.

Student 2

From: Year 11 Committee
To: Mr Smith, Headteacher
Purpose: To suggest ways in which facilities could be improved for Year 11 students

So far in Allerdale Comprehensive School there isn't much for Year 11 students. One way in which we could improve facilities is by creating a Year 11 common room. It would be a quiet place for students. There should also be a computer room for Year 11 to go. I think that there should be an unlimited amount of money for printing off. Another way in which you could improve the facilities is by having a separate canteen for them. In conclusion, I think that there are lots of suggestions for you to think about!

1 Do you think Student 2's report is better than Student I's report? Explain why/why not.

2 There are some good points about Student 2's report. List **two** strengths.

3 However, there are some negative points as well. Write down **two** weaknesses.

4 Highlight the ideas or sentences that you think could have been developed in more detail. Add any suggestions for improvement.

Activity 4

Below is a student report to the headteacher and governors about the possibility of creating a new school canteen. Read it very carefully and look at how the paragraphs have been organised and how subheadings have been used.

A report on the school canteen for the Headteacher and Governors of Allerdale School

Introduction

The school council has been asked by the headteacher and governors to put together a report on the condition, facilities and food in the school canteen. As a member of the council I have asked the opinion of other school students from different year groups and have included these in my findings.

1. Background

For many years the school canteen has been unable to cope with the vast number of hungry students hoping to be fed at lunchtime and as a result many leave the school premises to visit the local chip shop instead.

2. The benefits of having a new canteen

Teachers often complain that students are late for afternoon registration and lessons because they have left the premises for lunch. A larger, purpose-built canteen would stop this problem. There could be a larger section for a healthy salad bar with another for appetising hot food.

3. Where could we build the new canteen?

We could knock down the existing canteen and expand it to double the size by building on a section of the yard which is never actually used by students. This would allow the canteen to adequately cater for the 1500 students in the school during an hour lunch period. If we were to stagger the lunch breaks for the lower and middle school this would prove even more effective.

4. Helping to improve discipline

We know that as a headteacher discipline and the behaviour of students is always a high priority. By having a larger canteen, we will no longer have the problem of hungry, discontented students misbehaving in the corridors whilst waiting to be fed. Also students will no longer need to go off site for their lunch and consequently will not cause disruption to the general public.

Conclusion

We hope that you will see that creating a new school canteen is a good idea and we look forward to discussing the proposal in more detail at the next council meeting.

Jordan Hill
(President of the School Council)

1 Identify these features on the report. Write the correct feature letters in the boxes and use arrows to identify exactly where each feature is used.

a Examples of formal and clear language.

b A respectful and calm tone.

c Summing up the point of the report and suggesting what should happen next.

d Paragraphs divided by subheadings which consider different ideas.

e A short introductory paragraph to show why they are writing the report.

f A clear title where the audience and purpose are clearly established.

Activity 5

30 minutes

Now, using the previous report as a model example, try planning a report of your own. Read the exam question below.

Your school/college is considering ways in which it could improve the environment and save resources. You have been asked to write a report to the headteacher, suggesting action that could be taken. *(20 marks)*

Heading: _____

Introduction: _____

_____

_____

_____

Subheading 1: _____

_____

_____

_____

Subheading 2: _____

_____

_____

_____

Subheading 3: _____

_____

_____

_____

Conclusion: _____

_____

_____

_____

Here is another report written by a student in response to the exam question below.
Read the report together with the two examiner comments.

> **Write a report for the local council about the facilities available to young people in your area and how these could be improved.**
>
> *(20 marks)*

Student 1

This is a report to the local council about facilities in my area and how they can be improved. There are lots of things we need to improve because at the moment their arent many things for us. Usually on a night me and my friends have to go to the park and sit on the benchs because we cant afford the bus fair to go into town and the cinema costs a lot. We end up making a lot of nose because we havnt got nowhere to go and people call the police because they think we will cause truble. If we had a youth club or a sports hall were we culd go this wuldnt happen because we wuld have somthing to do.

I hope you read this report and do somthing about what I've said.

Yours sincerely

David Franklin

Examiner Comment 1

Content and organisation: There is a sense of purpose, however an incorrect format has been used. The ending is more appropriate for a letter but not a report. The student could have used subheadings and developed many of the points further. The tone is not always sufficiently formal ('me and my friends'), and overall it is much too short.

Sentence structure, punctuation and spelling: There are some paragraphs, and full stops are used. However, many words are misspelled (instances highlighted) and apostrophes omitted (instances highlighted).

Examiner Comment 2

Content and organisation: The response answers the question and there is a clear sense of audience, and purpose. The tone is friendly and the ideas are interesting and well developed.

Sentence structure, punctuation and spelling: The writing is fluent and well organised. The sentences are varied in length and the student's vocabulary is ambitious. Spelling and punctuation are very accurate.

1 Which examiner comment has been written about the report?

2 Why do you think this is the correct examiner comment?

3 What does the student need to do to improve the report to get a grade C? Read the criteria on page 48 to help you explain.

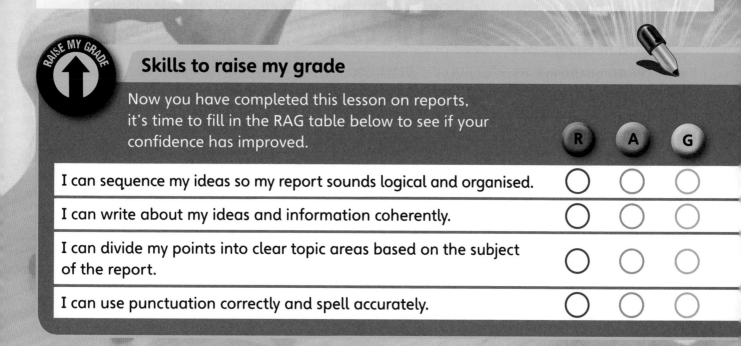

RAISE MY GRADE

Skills to raise my grade

Now you have completed this lesson on reports, it's time to fill in the RAG table below to see if your confidence has improved.

	R	A	G
I can sequence my ideas so my report sounds logical and organised.	○	○	○
I can write about my ideas and information coherently.	○	○	○
I can divide my points into clear topic areas based on the subject of the report.	○	○	○
I can use punctuation correctly and spell accurately.	○	○	○

10 Articles

Skills to raise my grade

Fill in the RAG table below to show how confident you are in the following areas:

	R	A	G
I can understand the features of an article.	○	○	○
I can put forward an opinion or information coherently.	○	○	○
I can use a variety of sentence structures and a range of vocabulary.	○	○	○
I can use punctuation correctly.	○	○	○

Top tips! Article writing

1 Your audience will usually be teenage magazine readers. Remember, if you are asked to write an article for a newspaper you will have to write in a slightly more formal way. In the exam you will be told who the audience will be.
2 Your purpose is generally to give information or put forward an opinion in an entertaining and lively way.
3 Your language will depend on the topic and audience, but generally it should be quite chatty.
4 Your tone will depend on the actual task, but it should usually be quite lively.
5 You will be expected to organise your writing in a clear and purposeful way:
   - **a heading** – as catchy as possible
   - **an introduction** – to grab the attention
   - **3–4 paragraphs** expanding your ideas and showing your viewpoint
   - **a short conclusion.**

Activity 1

10 minutes

A successful and interesting article will grab the attention of the reader immediately so that they will continue reading. To maintain this interest, writers use many techniques which are listed below.

Match each technique with its correct definition by drawing lines between the two.

Techniques	Definitions
Pun	The writing sounds relaxed and conversational
Sarcasm	A one-sided point of view
Imperative	A question where the answer is obvious
Ellipsis	Used to show excitement/shock/surprise or for emphasis
Informal tone	
Triple listing	Words which appeal to our feelings
Biased opinion	A technique to suggest everyone is involved
Alliteration	An order or command
Superlative	To build suspense or to show there is more to say …
Present tense	Speaking to the reader as an individual to make them feel involved
Exclamation	
Rhetorical question	Technique to make something sound personal
Emotive language	Using three words/adjectives to describe something
Exaggeration / hyperbole	Saying something is better/greater, etc. than it actually is
Second person direct appeal	An adjective describing something as the best, usually identified by having -est at the end of the adjective
First person singular – I	Words beginning with the same letter
First person plural – We	Writing as if something is happening now
	A play on words, a witty comment or a joke
	The use of mocking or ironic language

Activity 2

15 minutes

1 Look at the newspaper article 'The Beautiful Game' on pages 76–7. Write down what you think the **heading** tells us about the writer's attitude to football.

_____

_____

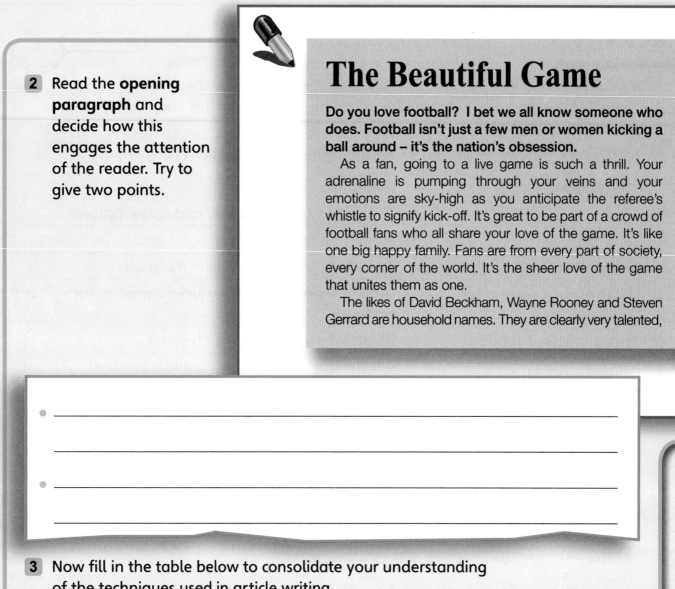

2 Read the **opening paragraph** and decide how this engages the attention of the reader. Try to give two points.

The Beautiful Game

Do you love football? I bet we all know someone who does. Football isn't just a few men or women kicking a ball around – it's the nation's obsession.

As a fan, going to a live game is such a thrill. Your adrenaline is pumping through your veins and your emotions are sky-high as you anticipate the referee's whistle to signify kick-off. It's great to be part of a crowd of football fans who all share your love of the game. It's like one big happy family. Fans are from every part of society, every corner of the world. It's the sheer love of the game that unites them as one.

The likes of David Beckham, Wayne Rooney and Steven Gerrard are household names. They are clearly very talented,

- _____
  _____

- _____
  _____

3 Now fill in the table below to consolidate your understanding of the techniques used in article writing.

Feature	Evidence	Effect
Rhetorical question		Draws the reader into the article as we begin to question ourselves and look for answers
Exaggeration		
Superlative		Nothing can beat the game of football
Triple listing	'They are clearly very talented, focused and skilful'	Emphasises the positive side of footballers' characters
Second person direct appeal		Makes reader feel directly involved as if article is aimed at him/her personally
Emotive words	'Passion', 'obsession', 'thrill'	

focused and skilful, transforming their passion on the pitch into first class football that their fans can be proud to support. But on the negative side, some footballers rake in more money in just one week than most of us earn in an entire year, and some of the top-flight footballers are unfortunately in the press more often for their activities off the pitch than on it.

Despite all the bad press (deserved or not) that some footballers receive, the majority of players are level-headed positive role models for many teenagers and young adults. Footballers need to constantly work on their fitness levels in order to perform well. They must be dedicated to their team, their coach and the game. So for them, football is not just a beautiful game – it's a way of life.

Activity 3

20 minutes

Now you have studied the techniques of article writing, try writing one of your own.

Read the exam question below.

> **Write a lively article for a teenage magazine about a well-known person you admire or dislike.**
>
> **(20 marks)**

You should aim to write a grade C article, so read the grade description on pages 48–9 before you begin.

1 First, think carefully and underline the key words in the question so you are clear about the audience, purpose and format of the task.

2 Now plan your work before you begin to write your article, and think of a heading to attract readers. Write your ideas here.

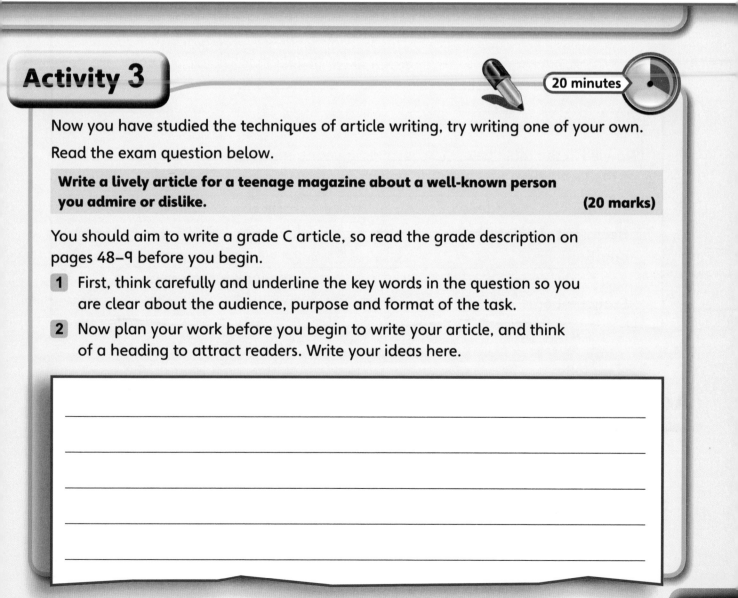

3 Write your article here.

_____

_____

_____

_____

_____

_____

_____

_____

_____

_____

_____

_____

_____

_____

_____

_____

_____

Activity 4

4 minutes

Look at your article. Highlight the features of article writing you have used based on the examples below.

Brief introduction   Persuasive techniques   Range of sentence lengths

Paragraphs   Short conclusion

1 Read this grade D student answer written in response to the exam question you answered in Activity 3.

D **grade answer**

Simon Cowell: Hero or Villain?

Everyone has an opinion about tvs mr nasty but does he deserve the bad press he receves? Simon Cowell is famous because he has a lot of money and hes on tele all the time. I like him because hes on the X factor and made Leona Lewis famous and I really like her type of singing. I think hes really good on the tele because he is honest and its funny when he starts quareling with Louis. My favourite Simon Cowell shows are X Factor, Britain's Got Talent and American Idol.

In the X factor the judges are Cheryl Cole, Dani Minogie and Louis Walsh but I like Cheryl the most because Girls Aloud are great. And anyway she always wins so she must be talented, even though some people think she mimes on stage!

2 Identify **three** ways in which you could make it a grade C.

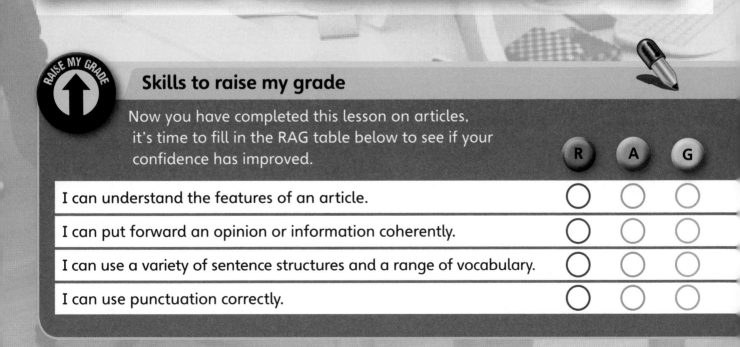

RAISE MY GRADE

Skills to raise my grade

Now you have completed this lesson on articles, it's time to fill in the RAG table below to see if your confidence has improved.

	R	A	G
I can understand the features of an article.	○	○	○
I can put forward an opinion or information coherently.	○	○	○
I can use a variety of sentence structures and a range of vocabulary.	○	○	○
I can use punctuation correctly.	○	○	○

11 Leaflets

Skills you need:

You must show that you can:
- understand and use the key features of writing leaflets
- plan and write a leaflet

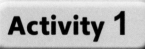

Skills to raise my grade

Fill in the RAG table below to show how confident you are in the following areas:

	R	A	G
I understand the key features of a leaflet.	○	○	○
I can use an appropriate layout for a leaflet.	○	○	○
I can organise my information in a clear and logical way.	○	○	○
I can express my information in a straightforward way.	○	○	○
I can spell and use punctuation correctly.	○	○	○

Activity 1

10 minutes

In order to check how much you know about writing a leaflet, complete the quiz below by ticking the correct answers.

1 What is a leaflet?
- **a** a list of words and their meanings written in alphabetical order ☐
- **b** a glossy brochure describing a place to go on holiday ☐
- **c** usually a piece of paper with a message to put across. ☐

2 What is the purpose of a leaflet?
- **a** to inform ☐
- **b** to entertain ☐
- **c** to persuade. ☐

3 Which **two** of these techniques are often found in the heading of a leaflet?
- **a** a question ☐
- **b** a long descriptive sentence ☐
- **c** second person direct appeal (you/your) ☐
- **d** a picture ☐
- **e** an application form. ☐

4 Sub headings are often used because...
- **a** they make the leaflet look more attractive ☐
- **b** they fill up the space ☐
- **c** they divide ideas clearly, making it easier for the reader to follow. ☐

What is the purpose of a leaflet?

Leaflets are usually written to **give information** and to **explain clearly** to a certain audience what you believe they need to know about a specific topic. Leaflets often have a **persuasive tone**.

Top tips! Writing leaflets

1 Always read the question carefully and underline the key words to decide on the purpose (**why** you are writing the leaflet) and the audience (**who** will read the leaflet).

2 Select only what is relevant and important.

3 Organise your facts/ideas clearly so the reader can understand easily. Remember to include a heading and subheadings/sections to divide your points logically.

4 Write your ideas in a clear and accurate way.

5 You are not expected to design and draw artistic pictures. If you want to show where you think a picture would be helpful, simply draw a box and write inside it what the picture would show.

6 Your audience will vary, but the exam paper will always make it clear which person, group of people or organisation your leaflet should be aimed at. This must influence what you include in your leaflet.

Activity 2

3 minutes

Read the leaflet entitled 'Drink, Drugs and Sausage Rolls' on page 82.

1 Highlight/underline and write around the leaflet the **layout** features that you can find.

2 Highlight/underline and write around the leaflet the **language** features that you can find.

3 Was this leaflet persuasive? Explain your answer.

DRINK, DRUGS & SAUSAGE ROLLS

Health and wellness programme

in association with
squareball

Don't let your good intentions put you in danger ... if you are jogging, cycling or walking regularly, try to vary your route and the time that you exercise. Always stick to well-lit roads, main paths or open spaces where you can be seen. Let someone know where you are going and what time you're expected back, and if possible keep your mobile phone on you. You can always use it to have the pizza delivered and waiting for when you get home...

www.ulster.gaa.ie

just the FACTS

Think that's an excuse?

There may be many reasons why you aren't currently taking exercise, but are these just excuses?

- Time – Schedule time for exercise between or after classes, or substitute some of your TV time for exercise.

- Money – Many fitness centres offer reduced membership for students, joining a team is free and it costs nothing to go for a walk!

- Boredom – Most gyms offer a wide range of classes for all interests – from circuits to salsa classes, so have a look around until you find something you will enjoy. Exercise to your favourite music or bring a friend along to make it a social occasion.

- Pain – Listen to what your body is telling you and if it hurts – STOP! Start slowly and increase your levels gradually.

- Embarrassment – Exercise may feel intimidating at first, but don't let this put you off. Other people in gyms are there to get fit, not to look at you! But if you really can't shake off the feeling, there are lots of exercises you can do at home where no one will see you!

- Tiredness – Exercise actually gives you more energy and will help you sleep better at night – both of which should help ease your tiredness.

Ulster Council GAA
8-10 Market Street, Armagh, BT61 7BX.
T: (028) 3752 1900 F: (028) 3752 8092
E: info@ulster.gaa.ie www.ulster.gaa.ie

In association with

www.squareball.com

Activity 3

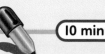

10 minutes

1 Read the leaflet 'Getting Active Feeling Fit' on page 84. Then match these features of leaflet writing to where they are demonstrated in the leaflet. Write the correct feature letter in the box and use arrows to identify exactly where each feature is used.

> **a** Paragraphs are short and clear
> **b** Clear title so that the purpose is immediately obvious
> **c** Illustrations to make the leaflet look attractive. If you want to show illustrations in your own leaflet, remember to simply draw a box and write in it what the picture will be
> **d** Instructions are simple and direct and the imperative is often used
> **e** Bullet points are often used when writing lists
> **f** The language is clear to understand
> **g** Helpful, practical advice is given
> **h** A memorable logo to identify the organisation
> **i** Immediate appeal to audience who will want to read the leaflet because they want to improve their lifestyle
> **j** Subheadings are used to divide up the ideas in the leaflet

2 What do you think are the **two** most successful features or word choices in this leaflet? Explain your choices.

getting *ACTIVE*

feeling *FIT*

The most effective way to achieve and maintain a healthy body shape is through a combination of physical activity and healthy eating (see below).

This should help you to maintain an energy balance, so that you are not taking in more energy through food than you are using in physical activity.

Strengthening exercises, such as weight training, circuit training, and body conditioning are also useful, as they tone and condition muscles at the same time.

The key to exercising for weight management is simply to be more active, more often. Any type of physical activity uses energy, so you should find ways to be more active in your everyday life.

Ideally aim to do at least 30 minutes of moderate intensity physical activity each day, for example:

- brisk walking
- swimming
- cycling
- dancing

we are what WE EAT

To start with, try making changes to your eating habits. For a well-balanced, healthy diet, choose a few things from the list. Introduce them into your diet, then gradually build in as many others as you can.

- fruit
- vegetables

Try to eat at least five portions of fruit and vegetables each day. Include some vegetables, some salad and some fruit. Choose a wide variety.

- meat, fish and alternatives

Choose lean meat or trim any visible fat. Remove the skin from poultry. Try to eat two portions of fish a week, especially oily fish such as mackerel or sardines.

- bread
- cereals
- potatoes

Make these foods the main part of your meals. Eat all types, and choose high-fibre varieties whenever you can.

- milk
- dairy foods

These are a good source of calcium. Choose lower-fat alternatives whenever you can.

- foods containing fat
- foods containing sugar

Try not to eat these too often. When you do eat them, have small amounts.

you can DO IT

Getting active simply means adjusting your lifestyle to make it more physical. Just 30 minutes of activity a day will bring benefits in terms of health, energy and general well-being. If you combine this with a healthy diet, you have the key to getting active and feeling fit.

Health Promotion Wales

Activity 4

20 minutes

Using the techniques you have revised in Activities 1–3, you are now going to plan and write a leaflet of your own, based on an example. The leaflet is to persuade teenagers to give up smoking.

1 Before you write your leaflet, think about:
- Who is it for? (audience)
- Why do they need it? (purpose)
- How friendly/formal/hard-hitting/ dramatic/serious should it be?

2 Now write your own leaflet here.

Activity 5

⏱ 3 minutes

Look at the leaflet you have written. How many of the following features have you included? Write an example of each of the features that you have used in your leaflet in the table below.

Remember that using these techniques will help you achieve a grade C.

Feature	✓ or ✗	Example from your leaflet
A headline		
A picture		
Direct appeal		
Relaxed, colloquial language		
Scientific facts or words		
Frightening statistics		
Dramatic, emotive words to scare the reader		
Imperatives or commands		
Some encouragement or practical, helpful hints		

GradeStudio

⏱ 10 minutes

1 Read the following student leaflet which has been marked at grade C.

Student 1

<u>You are what you eat!</u>

So many people these days concider eating fruit around school as being uncool.
However I want to show you that it's not.
Do you recognise these people?

Would you consider these people as being uncool?
If all of these famous sports players are eating fruit then why
aren't we? Could eating healthily be the key to their success?

(a picture – famous sportspeople eating fruit before a game)

Continued ...

It has been proven that eating two bananas before exercise could give you enough energy for a very hard 90 minute workout. If you turn on the TV to a sports channel you will never see a sportsman or woman eating a bag of crisps. It will always be a banana or sandwhich to raise their energy levels and stay healthy at the same time.

<u>Did you have a hard day at school?</u>
It has been proven that if you eat a very healthy breakfast before school then you will perform better during class or whilst doing sporting activities. Eating healthily in the morning will increase your energy level and you will concentrate and focus for longer.
If you love to take part in sport a healthy diet with all the food groups is essential, it allows the body to gain all the nutrients that are needed for the days activities. It will also result in a healthier fitter life.

2   Identify where the answer has met the grade C mark scheme using the table below.

Grade C criteria	Example of this in the grade C answer
• A clear heading to catch the attention of the reader	
• An introduction which explains what it is about	
• Subheadings for separate points so that it is easy to read	
• Clear facts and information so the leaflet is useful	
• A picture	

Skills to raise my grade

Now you have completed this lesson on leaflets, it's time to fill in the RAG table below to see if your confidence has improved.

	R	A	G
I understand the key features of a leaflet.	○	○	○
I can use an appropriate layout for a leaflet.	○	○	○
I can organise my information in a clear and logical way.	○	○	○
I can express my information in a straightforward way.	○	○	○
I can spell and use punctuation correctly.	○	○	○

Skills you need:

You must show that you can:
- understand and use the key features of writing speeches
- plan and write a speech effectively

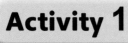

Skills to raise my grade

Fill in the RAG table below to show how confident you are in the following areas:

	R	A	G
I know what the key features of a speech are.	○	○	○
I can use an appropriate layout when I am writing a speech.	○	○	○
I can use persuasive techniques effectively to convince my audience about my ideas in a speech.	○	○	○
I can organise and express my information in a clear and logical way.	○	○	○
I can use punctuation accurately and spell correctly.	○	○	○

Activity 1

3 minutes

In order to check how much you know about writing a speech, read the following statements and decide whether each one is true or false.

Statement	True or false
1 The purpose of a speech is usually to persuade the audience	
2 A speech needs a powerful and important opening point in order to grab the interest and attention of the audience	
3 I do not need to introduce myself to my audience at the start of my speech	
4 When I write my speech I need to use subheadings	
5 I need to use persuasive techniques to make my audience agree with me	
6 Using a question is a good way of making my audience think about what I am saying	
7 I should keep my least important point until the end of my speech	

Top tips! Speech writing

1 Always read the question carefully and underline the key words to decide on the purpose (**why** you are making the speech) and the audience (**who** will hear it).

2 In the exam, this piece of writing may be called a talk or a phone-in speech. You should tackle these questions in exactly the same way as a speech.

3 Your purpose will usually be to persuade an audience to agree with what you are saying.

4 Make sure you have lots of good ideas and use forceful, persuasive language to sweep your listeners along with you.

5 Your audience will vary, but the exam paper will always make clear which person, group of people or organisation your speech is aimed at. This must influence what you include in your speech.

6 Remember that an audience will only hear your speech once, so organise your ideas into the best possible order.

7 Your tone needs to be forceful but polite. Try to use as many persuasive techniques as you can.

Activity 2

15 minutes

1 Read the three extracts from three different speeches that follow. Highlight/underline and write down the language features that you can find in the speeches.

Speech 1

Ladies and gentlemen,

I am here this evening to persuade you that we must abolish school uniform and put an end to this outdated and unnecessary custom.

School uniform is old fashioned! Do you ever stop to think when you take your son or daughter to buy yet another regulation black jumper that you are stifling their individuality, free choice and self expression? We have been teenagers ourselves, ladies and gentlemen, and surely we all remember the discomfort of wearing stiff shirt collars and ties. Should we really inflict this needless torture on the next generation?

Speech 2

I am here today to convince you that keeping animals in zoos and circuses is both inhumane and wrong.

Majestic kings of the jungle are locked up in small cages only to be paraded for the amusement of tourists! Surely, as sensitive and caring individuals, you have to agree with me that this cruelty to beautiful and wild creatures must be stopped!

Speech 3

Hello listeners. My name is Ben and after hearing the previous caller's ludicrous claims, I felt I had to give my opinion and stand up for the youth of today.

The younger generation are continuously under scrutiny and criticised with the sweeping generalisation that they are all selfish, lazy and unemployed layabouts who do nothing except drink and hang around aimlessly causing trouble in town centres. I can assure you that this is certainly NOT the case!

2 Choose one of the speech extracts above and try to write the next paragraph to develop the argument logically. Remember to use some persuasive techniques and to write accurately and carefully.

_____
_____
_____
_____
_____
_____
_____
_____
_____
_____
_____
_____
_____

Activity 3

10 minutes

Read the opening of this speech about raising the age limit for driving to 21.

Match these features of speech-writing to where they are demonstrated in the speech. Write the correct feature letter in the box and use arrows to identify exactly where each feature is used.

a Clear opening statement so that your audience knows what you are talking about

b Rhetorical question to involve the audience directly and make them think about the point

c Paragraphs are used effectively to show the ideas are organised. Remember you don't need subheadings

d Makes the opening point clearly

e Moves on to the second point in the argument smoothly

f Another rhetorical question to keep the audience interested

g Emotive and persuasive language

I am speaking in favour of the driving age to be raised to 21. This would be an unpopular decision among young people, but it would be a very good idea for the wider public. Basically, there are two reasons – safety and finance.

First, safety. Government figures show that accidents involving young drivers are out of all proportion to the number of young drivers on the road. Your drivers and passengers are regularly involved in tragedies, when all four (or more) youngsters die instantly in a head-on crash at speed, How often have we read of someone passing their test and driving recklessly immediately after? They need protecting from themselves. Speed is the temptation – the opportunity to show off to your mates or to impress a new girlfriend, without thinking for a minute of what damage you can do to yourself and others, including those innocent people in other cars or walking along the street. Raising the driving age limit to 21 would remove peer-group pressure, because if your friend has a car, then another friend, then you want one too.

This brings me on to the second point, money. How can every young person hope to afford to buy a car when they are still at school, college or university or they are unemployed? Surely parents can't be expected to pay for an extra car? Many of the cars that young people drive are bangers and they are not roadworthy – another reason why so many accidents take place. It would be better for the law to be changed so that young people can actually save or spend their money on other safer things.

Activity 4

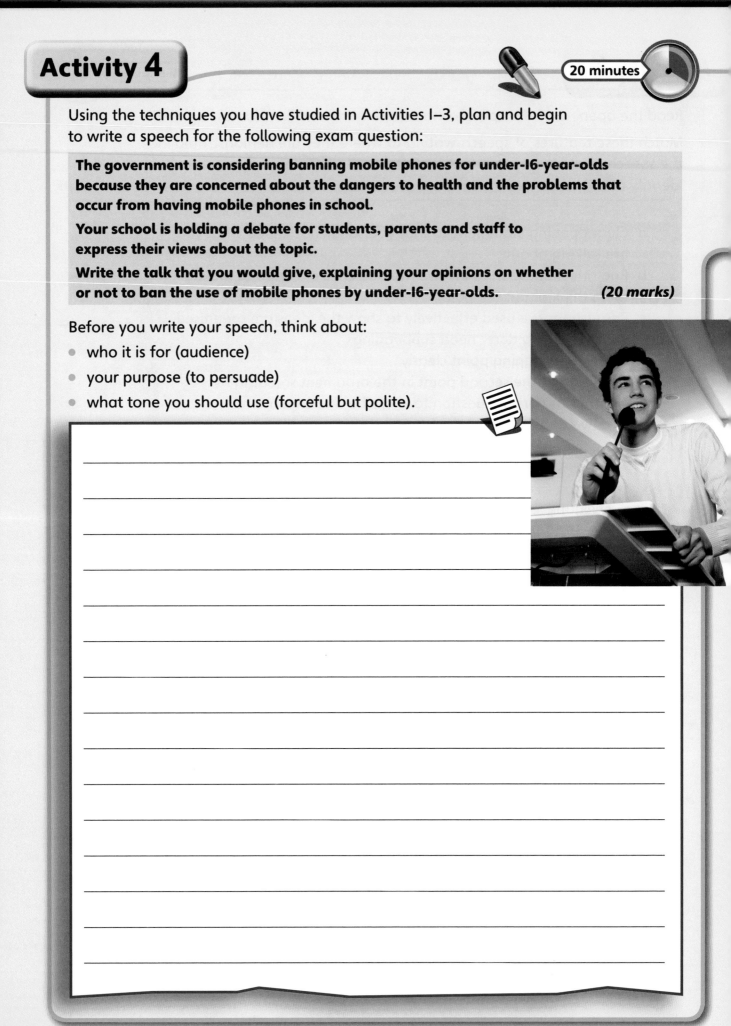

20 minutes

Using the techniques you have studied in Activities 1–3, plan and begin to write a speech for the following exam question:

> **The government is considering banning mobile phones for under-16-year-olds because they are concerned about the dangers to health and the problems that occur from having mobile phones in school.**
>
> **Your school is holding a debate for students, parents and staff to express their views about the topic.**
>
> **Write the talk that you would give, explaining your opinions on whether or not to ban the use of mobile phones by under-16-year-olds.**   *(20 marks)*

Before you write your speech, think about:

- who it is for (audience)
- your purpose (to persuade)
- what tone you should use (forceful but polite).

_____

_____

_____

Activity 5

3 minutes

Look at the speech you wrote in Activity 4. How many of the following features have you included? Remember that using these techniques will help you achieve that grade C.

Feature	✓ or ✗	Example from your speech
Introducing myself		
Strong opening paragraph		
Dramatic/persuasive/ emotive words		
Exclamations		
Rhetorical questions		
Figures and statistics		
Flattering audience		
Second person direct appeal		
Strong conclusion		
Polite ending		
Paragraphs used carefully		
Accurate spelling		

1 Read the grade descriptions on pages 48–9, then read the extracts from three different speeches that follow. Match them with the correct grade descriptions using the table opposite.

Speech 1

I am a fifteen year old teenager and I would like to give my opinion about if the legal drinking age should be 18 not 21.
Lots of teenagers are involved in fatal drink driving incidents as they have not become responsible as they should. I feel that parents are unaware of what their children are doing on nights out. If the age is raised to 21, then they will have had four years of driving experience behind them and will be more mature. I think we would see a lot less drink driving accidents.

Speech 2

My name is sarah and I am phoning in to say that it is hard to be a teenager because parents and teachers don't know what its like to be us and they dont understand all what we have to cope with like school and exams and friends and worrying if we will have jobs. Thank you for listening to me

Speech 3

I am phoning into your show to reply to the comment that all young people are selfish, lazy layabouts. In my opinion this is simply not true and this person obviously has a prejudiced and stereotyped view of young people today!
Nowadays young people receive a lot of bad press and media coverage and this fuels the fire for Britain's prejudice and growing hatred. The young people who do not enjoy getting into trouble with the law or binge drinking receive less press therefore not being able to redeem the name of Britain's youngsters.

Speech	Grade description	Why have you matched this speech with this grade description?	What grade would you award this speech?
1			
2			
3			

Skills to raise my grade

Now you have completed this lesson on speeches, it's time to fill in the RAG table below to see if your confidence has improved.

	R	A	G
I know what the key features of a speech are.	○	○	○
I can use an appropriate layout when I am writing a speech.	○	○	○
I can use persuasive techniques effectively to convince my audience about my ideas in a speech.	○	○	○
I can organise and express my information in a clear and logical way.	○	○	○
I can use punctuation accurately and spell correctly.	○	○	○

Reviews

Skills you need:

You must show that you can:
- understand and use key features of review writing
- plan and write a review effectively

Skills to raise my grade

Fill in the RAG table below to show how confident you are in the following areas:

	R	A	G
I understand the key features of reviews.	○	○	○
I can use an appropriate layout for a review.	○	○	○
I can give a sensible opinion of the topic being reviewed.	○	○	○
I can organise and express my information in a clear and straightforward way.	○	○	○
I can use punctuation accurately and spell correctly.	○	○	○

Top tips! Reviews

1 Always read the question carefully and underline the key words to decide on the purpose (why you are writing the review) and the audience (who will read it).

2 Your review should be written in paragraphs and should finish with your opinion/recommendation of the topic being reviewed.

3 The purpose of writing a review is to pass on information to the reader by giving your opinion of the item you are reviewing, whether it be a film, book, CD or concert.

4 If you are reviewing a film or book, do not to retell what happens because this will spoil the ending for the viewer/reader.

5 Your audience will vary, but the exam paper will always make clear which person, group of people or organisation your review is aimed at. This must influence the tone of your review.

6 A review should be written in organised paragraphs. You should begin by stating the title of the item you are reviewing and using this as a heading. Subheadings may be used.

7 You should always finish with your opinion and a recommendation, and you may include a star rating.

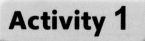

Activity 1

5 minutes

In order to write a good review, you need to think carefully about the words you use and the effect they would have on your audience.

1 Look at these lists of adjectives that are frequently used in review writing. Decide whether each word would give a **positive** or **negative** impression of the film/book/CD being reviewed and write your answer in the table below.

Word	Positive or negative
Engaging	
Boring	
Entertaining	
Gripping	
Slow paced	
Unrealistic	
Interesting	
Lively	
Action packed	
Unoriginal	
Frustrating	
Enjoyable	
Convincing	
Thrilling	
Dreadful	
Dire	

2 Now try to think of six adjectives, or describing words, of your own choice that could be used in review writing, and decide whether each one creates positive or negative impressions.

Your adjective	Positive or negative

Activity 2

15 minutes

Read the two reviews that follow: '*Step Up* 3D' and 'Westlife Concert Experience'.

1 For both reviews, highlight and annotate the following:
- layout/format features
- language features, including positive and negative words.

Step Up 3D review (12A)
Bit of a step down, to be honest.
BY: Emma Dibdin Aug 2 2010

Step Up **3D review:** All Moose (Adam G. Sevani, poor man's Jesse Eisenberg) wants to do is dance. He wants to dance more than he wants to attend classes at NYU, own the newest product-placed Nike footwear, or notice the affections of equally awkward bezza Camille (Alyson Stoner).

A spontaneous street-dancing incident (who hasn't been there?) leads him to a meeting with brooding malcontent Luke (Rick Malambri, poor man's Channing Tatum) who happens to head up a ragtag crew of misfits and rebels all with one thing in common: their insatiable appetite to dance.

And they do. In fairness, they do it well, with choreography one of the saving graces in this mishmash of half-boiled characterisations, pumping bass choons and gaudy 3D antics.

Verdict:
There are moments of energetic charm here, but the script is so painfully poor, and the plot's creaky turns so unintentionally comedic, that they're all but lost in the noise.

Worldpop.com

Westlife Concert Experience
Venue: Wembley Arena (London)
Date: March, 10, 2001
Rating: ★ ★ ★ ☆ ☆

The familiar piano intro… and banish it from your mind. Westlife's live show is anything but predictable. They do play upbeats, they do dance and there isn't a stool in sight. The live vocals are outstanding, with Mark in particular proving he is far and away the best singer in the group. There are great moments: 'Swear It Again', a cappella version of 'My Girl' and the show-closing rendition of 'Flying Without Wings' while suspended above the heads of the crowds, to name but a few. However, Westlife's concert suffers from its self-conscious attempt to emulate other pop shows. While endeavouring to recreate the spectacle of Backstreet Boys or 'N Sync, Westlife find themselves erring on the wrong side of bizarre: they start the show by being awoken from the dead, they do 'Uptown Girl' dressed as Kwik Fit Fitters and they perform 'Seasons In The Sun' on a moving treadmill while removing their jackets, detachable sleeve by detachable sleeve, stripper style! It seems Westlife are so concerned about proving the critics wrong with their dance routines, they've forgotten where their talent really lies. A perfect Westlife concert would be exactly what everyone expects, their best ballads sung live with a live band, minus the dancers – after all, no Westlife fan wants to see other girls flirting with her idols. Why try to be another BSB when they do it so well? Westlife are great live performers, it's just a shame their live show (if you'll pardon the pun) falls between too many stools.

2 Which of the two reviews do you think is the most effective?
Give a reason for your choice.

Activity 3

10 minutes

Read this review of the book *Twilight*. Match these features of review writing to where they are demonstrated in the review. Write the correct feature letter in the box and use arrows to identify exactly where each feature is used.

a Weaknesses as well as strengths are written about
b Personal opinion and recommendation of the book
c Subheadings not used but paragraphs follow on logically
d Heading
e Details of plot keep reader interested but do not give away the ending
f Opening paragraph introducing the book and giving some information about the characters and plot

Twilight by Stephenie Meyer – Book Review

Twilight is told by 17-year-old Bella Swan, who moves from Phoenix to the small town of Forks, Washington, to live with her dad for the remainder of high school. There, she meets Edward Cullen and his family, who possess an other-worldly and irresistible beauty and grace to which Bella is drawn. *Twilight* is the tale of Bella and Edward's burgeoning relationship, brimming with standard teenage drama alongside the unexpected, because, after all, Edward and his family are vampires. These undead friends have chosen to deny their urge to drink blood, instead slaking their thirst with the blood of animals. Bella soon finds out, however, that not all vampires in her life are constrained by such scruples.

The book has been praised for its treatment of sexuality and morality. Although there's plenty of yearning and sensuality, there is no sex, drinking, or drug use. Edward refuses Bella's desire to be turned into a vampire herself, on grounds that it wouldn't be the right thing to do.

Twilight is an easy and enjoyable read. Its first-person viewpoint keeps the pages turning. This isn't a masterpiece of literary achievement, however, you have to take it for what it is – a unique and entertaining, if not flawlessly written, story. *Twilight* will almost certainly appeal to teenage girls and many women of all ages, but probably not to the majority of males. It's sure to make readers eager to devour the next three novels.

Activity 4

30 minutes

Using all the techniques you have studied and revised in this lesson, plan and write a review in response to the following exam question.

Write a review for a teenage audience of either your favourite film or CD. *(20 marks)*

Before you write your review, think about:
- who it is for (teenage audience)
- your purpose (to inform and give a sensible and considered opinion)
- what tone you should use (entertaining and relaxed).

1 Write your plan here.

2 Now write your review.

Activity 5

5 minutes

Look at the review you wrote in Activity 4 and read the grade descriptions on pages 48–9.

1 Which grade is your review closer to? Write your own examiner comment to explain how your writing matches the grade you have awarded yourself.

Read the following reviews, written by students in exam conditions in response to the question below.

> **Write a review aimed at teenagers about a film or music of your choice.** *(20 marks)*

C grade answer

This latest album released by Prince entitled 'the genius' is a well made mix of both previous hits and new titles from the once un-named musician.

With the ability to play nearly every musical instrument knows to man, and the imagination to write and compose all of his own songs, talent is one thing that cannot be criticised. Prince Rodgers Nelson is known as one of the all time great in the music industry for both the film and album 'Purple Rain'. This contains such tracks included in his new album.

The latest tracks on the genius however are vastly different from those that his fans know and admire. Nearly all the slow beat, slow tempo love ballads seem to express the exact same emotions and feelings as each other with similar lyrics. All are disappointing and lifeless that make you feel and think about turning the stereo off rather than fantasise about the joy of love and romance. The albums' one saving grace are perhaps the timeless classics included on the album such as 'Kiss', 'When Doves Cry' and '1999'. The title definitely does not reflect the latest material on this album. This is a tragic let down to Prince fans everywhere.

The girly looking, heel wearing musician who once had legions of fans worldwide will surely be missed as this is not the same man as people around the world in the early eighties till the mid nineties came to love. Maybe a career change or possibly retirement will suit Prince more.

Overall, an agonising 2/10. We at Youth Music Magazine advise you not to purchase this album. If you are a Prince fan, buy his greatest hits album.

D grade answer

Save the Last dance is a film about a girl pursuing her dream to become a dancer. Unfortunetly her luck changes when on the day of her audition her mum doesn't turn up to support her. Sarah is upset stud doesnt understand why her mum would want to upset her by not turning up. After tripping up and falling in the audition a police officer turns up to tell her that while her mum was driving to the audition she was killed in a car crash. Sarah then

has to move in with her father. She won't dance anymore as it hurts her too much when she thinks of her mum. But when she goes to her new school she meets new friends and falls for Derek. He then persuades her too dance again suddenly her dream doesn't seem such a lifetime away. This film is mainly about music, although it does have scenes of violence. I enjoyed the film because it gave the perspective of a dancer living in the 21st century. The film was set in Los Angelees, in the present day. Although the film was about dance there was a lot of romance so I would call this a romantic film. Sarah is the main character of the film; she seems so naeeve at the start, but once she started making friends you can clearly see that she is strong. At the end of the film they finally accept her as a white girl living in a black community. Derek is Sarah's best friends brother. He is inteligent and wants to be a doctor when he gets older. But his best friend is on the wrong side of the law, what Derek doesn't realise until the end of the film is that fighting doesn't solve anything. I would reccommend anyone who is intrested in dance to watch this film.

1 Imagine you are the examiner. What comments would you write about each answer, including the strengths and weaknesses in the areas of content and accuracy?

_____

_____

_____

_____

Skills to raise my grade

RAISE MY GRADE ↑

Now you have completed this lesson on review writing, it's time to fill in the RAG table below to see if your confidence has improved.

	R	A	G
I understand the key features of reviews.	○	○	○
I can use an appropriate layout for a review.	○	○	○
I can give a sensible opinion of the topic being reviewed.	○	○	○
I can organise and express my information in a clear and straightforward way.	○	○	
I can use punctuation accurately and spell correctly.	○	○	

Revision checklist WJEC GCSE English and English Language

Do you remember filling in this checklist at the beginning of your revision?

How confident do you feel about each of the areas below now that you have revised?

Fill in the revision checklist below.
- Tick green if you feel confident about this topic.
- Tick amber if you know some things, but revision will help to make your knowledge and skills the best they can be.
- Tick red if you are not confident about two or more aspects of this topic.

Remember to ask your teacher for help if you are unsure of any area.

RAISE MY GRADE

Unit 1: Reading non-fiction texts	R	A	G
1 Find and list questions	○	○	○
2 Impressions	○	○	○
3 Viewpoint and attitude	○	○	○
4 Intended audience	○	○	○
5 Analysis of persuasive techniques	○	○	○
6 Comparison of texts	○	○	○
Unit 2: Writing information and ideas			
7 Informal letters	○	○	○
8 Formal letters	○	○	○
9 Reports	○	○	○
10 Articles	○	○	○
11 Leaflets	○	○	○
12 Speeches	○	○	○
13 Reviews	○	○	○

If you are still unsure about a few areas, don't worry.
You still have time to ask your teacher for help and advice.
Good luck!

What your GCSE exam paper looks like

GCSE

**English Language
Foundation Tier**

Unit 1: Studying written language

1 hour

ADDITIONAL MATERIALS

A 12 page answer booklet

Resource Material

INSTRUCTIONS TO CANDIDATES

Answer **all** questions.

Write your answers in the separate answer
book provided.

INFORMATION FOR CANDIDATES

The number of marks is given in brackets at the
end of each question or part-question.

Reading Paper

The front cover will always remind
you how long you have to complete
the whole paper (1 hour). You must
decide how best to divide up your time
in order to read the material carefully
and answer all of the questions.

Ideally you should spend about 12 minutes
reading all the material very carefully and
making any notes you think may help you
to answer the questions.

You should then aim to spend 12 minutes
answering each question. Remember to
focus on the correct area of the text and
underline the key words in the question.

Remember to answer all the questions on
the paper and read through your answers
carefully before the end of the exam.

For English, these papers will be
called 'English in the Daily World'.

Writing Paper

The front cover will always remind you
how long you have to complete the
whole paper (1 hour). It will always
suggest that you divide your time
equally between the two questions
(about 30 minutes on each question).

Check your answers carefully before the
end of the exam because 7 marks on
each question are given for sentence
structure, punctuation and spelling.

Remember to answer both the
questions and aim to write about one
and a half sides in your answer booklet
for each question.

**English Language
Foundation Tier**

Unit 2: Using written language

1 hour

ADDITIONAL MATERIALS

A 12 page answer booklet

Resource Material

INSTRUCTIONS TO CANDIDATES

Answer **all** questions.

Write your answers in the separate answer
book provided.

You are advised to spend your time as follows:
Q.1 – about 30 minutes
Q.2 – about 30 minutes

INFORMATION FOR CANDIDATES

The number of marks is given in brackets at the
end of each question or part-question.

Sample exam paper

Reading paper

*Answer **all** the following questions.*

***The Resource Material** is from a website brochure produced by Astley Woods, a company which runs activity holidays.*

The second article, 'Astley Woods – holiday review', appeared on the Internet.

Look at Text 1, the Astley Woods website brochure.

1. List **ten** outdoor activities mentioned in the brochure that are available at Astley Woods. [10]

2. How does the website brochure try to persuade readers that an Astley Woods holiday is good for both children and parents? [10]

Now look at Text 2, the article 'Astley Woods – holiday review'.

3. What are the writer's thoughts and feelings about an Astley Woods holiday?

    You should include:
    *   what the writer liked;
    *   what the writer did not like;
    *   the writer's overall impression. [10]

You should now use details and information <u>from both texts</u> to answer the following question:

4. Both of these texts are about Astley Woods. Compare and contrast them, using the following headings:

    *   the accommodation at Astley Woods;
    *   the restaurants at Astley Woods;
    *   the Astley Woods settings. [10]

Text I

Astley Woods
'Action Plus' Holidays

Why choose an Astley Woods 'Action Plus' Holiday? Maybe you want a holiday that pushes you to the limit. Or you have children who enjoy trying their hand at new, exciting activities. An 'Action Plus' holiday delivers excitement and challenge for all. But if you would rather enjoy more gentle pursuits in locations of wonderful natural beauty, Astley Woods holiday centres can offer that too.

Enjoy the breeze when you sail across the lake, or join one of our woodland walks with our friendly Tracker Guides. And if you are looking for more challenge, you could always try the Log Swing, the High Tree Trek or the Zip Wire Challenge. Whatever you want from a holiday, Astley Woods works tirelessly to offer 'Action Plus' holidays that will leave you with the warm glow of personal achievement and of time well spent in beautiful natural surroundings.

Astley Woods also provides superb accommodation for your holiday. We offer our standard 'Wychwood Forest' chalets for guests who simply want to enjoy the huge range of facilities available at our sites. For guests who want to be pampered, we offer our 'New Forest' chalets which are exclusively designed and stylishly furnished to the highest standards, and include en-suite bathrooms and saunas.

Children's 'Action Plus' Holidays

Whether it's inside or outdoors, your children will have plenty of activities to choose from. Outside, they can enjoy the soccer schools, abseiling and paintballing, whilst inside there are activities like fashion-design, movie-making and DJing. Every age and interest is catered for and because our emphasis is on safety and on fun, you can be sure that you can relax when they are letting off steam.

Astley Woods Family Holidays

With their location, in 300 acres of unspoilt natural forest, the Astley Woods holiday centres offer a great choice of outdoor activities for all the family and for groups of all ages. We have something for everyone: from horse-riding to archery and from bird-watching to canoeing. Our instructors are all highly qualified and will help build your confidence and skill, whether you're an expert or beginner, ensuring your enjoyment whatever activity you choose.

We know that after a day spent exploring, playing or just relaxing, you'll want to enjoy a family meal together. We offer a range of superb restaurants and bistros where you can do just that, re-living the experiences of the day in a relaxed atmosphere. Each of our centres has a variety of themed restaurants, and with menus from every continent, we're sure that you'll feel spoilt for choice.

Memories to cherish forever

A children's 'Action Plus' holiday will give all the family the opportunity to spend precious time together, as well as offering your children a range of supervised activities that will mean they'll never get bored the whole time they're with us. We also make sure that whilst they are enjoying themselves, you can have time for yourself, either to make the most of the facilities on offer, or to just relax in the delightful surroundings.

There's so much more to keep them entertained at Astley Woods holiday centres than they could ever manage to do in just a single visit, so they're sure to pester you for another visit. We hope you'll share their wish to return again and again.

Text 2

Astley Woods

Holiday Review

The appeal of Astley Woods is that it is 'in the wild'. Actually, their sites are pretty much in the middle of nowhere, though this is sold as an attraction because you can 'get away from it all'. To be fair, the site we visited was set in glorious woodland with lots of nature trails and plenty of wildlife to try and spot.

There are a number of choices in accommodation to suit your budget. At the bottom of the price range is the 'Wychwood Forest' chalet, up to the most expensive 'New Forest' chalets that have things like a DVD in the cabin, private parking, and their own hot tub. The chalets are not the most attractive wooden buildings, but ours was clean and homely, although I heard one visitor complain that her chalet had a fusty smell and had dirty marks on the walls and doors. On arrival one of the first things I recommend is getting down to the Woods Market, which is a reasonably priced, well-stocked shop that sells freshly baked goods and the range of food that you're likely to find in small supermarkets.

One of the problems with Astley Woods is that it can get quite expensive, depending on what you want to do. It's true that it can be a relatively cheap week if you're happy just going to the pool, walking round the site and eating in. However, if you want to try your hand at the kinds of activities that are on offer, they do not come cheap. For example, quad biking was £35 for an hour and massages were £30 for 30 minutes. Activities I would recommend are the horse-riding lessons and the archery, which I really enjoyed, but it's advisable to book activities in advance, because the popular ones get booked up very quickly.

There's lots to do and many of the activities are suitable for children or those with families. You can also hire bikes, and it was good to be able to cycle all around the site and on the nature trails, though I thought £22 each for a bike (Mon–Fri) was very expensive. Another problem was that the bikes all looked similar so do try to remember where you park – one day I spent half an hour looking round trying to find my bike.

One annoying thing for me about the two Astley Woods centres I visited was that they seemed to be constantly under construction. I imagine this is kept to a minimum in peak season but as a visitor going in the cheap season I found various problems such as roads in the centre closed off and for two days the pool was shut down for maintenance.

The restaurants have varied menus and plenty of choices, but they are all quite expensive. One of the complaints I heard from visitors was that the restaurants often seemed to be under-staffed, and there were grumbles about slow service.

So is it worth it? Well, if you love swimming and hanging about a pool I suppose it is pretty good. Walking or cycling round the park is enjoyable except for all the noisy people, which doesn't quite match the tranquil image presented in the Astley Woods brochure. Overall, it is probably worth going to one of the centres for a few days away if you have never been before, and it's good if you have children and are willing to pay – quite a lot – for some of the extra things on offer. Having done it once though, I'm not sure I'd go back.

Writing paper

Answer Question 1

In this section you will be assessed for your writing skills, including the presentation of your work. Take special care with handwriting, spelling, punctuation and layout.

Think about the purpose, audience and, where appropriate, the format for your writing.

A guide to the amount you should write is given at the end of each question.

1. The notice below has been put up on your school/college notice board.

Active Breaks – Staff wanted

Active Breaks is a company that runs play-schemes for children in the 3–10 age range, and we're looking to recruit extra part-time staff for the school summer holidays.

We are looking for people who:
- work well with children in this age range
- can work as part of a team
- can carry out a variety of tasks.

If you are interested, please send your letter of application to:

Active Breaks – Recruitment
Tower House
Chester Road
Surrey
GU7 4LY

You decide to apply for one of the jobs available.

Write your letter of application. [20]

The quality of your writing is more important than its length. You should write about one to two pages in your answer book.

Personal notes and reminders

You may want to use this page to write down your personal revision targets, as well as any useful hints and tips you have learnt during your revision lessons to make your revision successful.